PN   G▢▢ ▢i▢▢▢el.
                    ▢rself!

Present Yourself!

By Michael J. Gelb

Jalmar Press
Rolling Hills Estates, CA

Jalmar Press
45 Hitching Post Drive, Bldg. 2
Rolling Hills Estates, CA 90274-4297

Library of Congress Cataloging-in-Publication Data

Gelb, Michael J.
Present Yourself!

Summary: Covers how to captivate your audience
with great presentation skills.
Includes sections on transforming fear,
knowing your audience, setting the stage,
making them remember, mind-mapping, body language,
visualization, relaxation and many others.

[1. Presentation Skills   2. Non-fiction   3. Mind-mapping]
I. Title   II. Title: Present Yourself!
Library of Congress Catalog Card Number: 88-80768
ISBN: Hardcover: 0-915190-50-8
Trade Paper: 0-915190-51-6
Printing: 10 9 8 7 6 5 4 3 2 1

This book is dedicated to Tony Buzan.

Contents

All Presentations Are Brain-Based
'Left Brain' Bias
Whole-Brained Presentations
Summary

The Trouble with Outlining
Mind Mapping: An Introduction
Mind Mapping Your Presentation
The Advantages of Mind Mapping
Summary

Know Your Audience
Intelligence Gathering
Set Your Objectives
Summary

Forty Word Memory Exercise
Your Audience's Memory
The Five Keys to Audience Recall
Vital Information—Timing and Breaks
Summary

Acknowledgements

Many thanks to the following people who have contributed to the creation of this book: Ann Darby Hutchinson, Beret Arcaya, Ed Bassett, the Gelbs (especially Joan) and the Kendalls, Shelley Liebman, Suzanne Nelson, Vanda North, Mike Rozek, Carla Siegel, Susan Southard, Ake Wilsby, Brad Winch, Ellen Wingard and Connie Zweig.

And special thanks to:

Leslie Traub, whose creativity, editorial expertise, feedback, love and support were essential to the creation of this book;

Tony Buzan, creator of Mind-Mapping, renaissance man and endless source of inspiration; and

Nancy Margulies, illustrator extraordinaire and all around creative genius.

Foreword

Once in a while a new book appears that transforms the way we look at a familiar subject.

The subject is presentation skills.

The book is *Present Yourself!* by Michael J. Gelb.

In business, in education and throughout the professions, presentation skills have become essential to advancement. The book you now hold in your hand offers you an original perspective on developing those skills.

Present Yourself! is the first book on presentation skills to be brain based; that is, considering in detail the brain-needs of the presenter and the brain-needs of the audience. In this way, the author has captured the essential elements necessary to any communicator, while at the same time considering the needs of every listener.

Present Yourself! is the first book on presentation skills to combine the pioneering work of F. Mathias Alexander on appropriate body use with my own work on the nature of creativity, memory, thinking and the new method of accessing your own intelligence, Mind Mapping.

Present Yourself! is also the first book on presentation skills that simultaneously gives you information on how to present, while providing an ongoing program of self-development.

In the true sense of the word 'liberation', Michael Gelb provides you with information that allows you an easy, step-by-step process to liberate your natural charisma; to discover the true communicator, the true genius, the *actual* you.

As the book is unique, so is Michael Gelb uniquely qualified to write it. Throughout the world, he has lectured and presented to audiences of all sizes (ranging from 1 to 250,000), all levels (ranging from the severely brain-damaged and disadvantaged to the highest levels of academia) and to those practicing in all the major areas of business, education and the professions. His clarity of expression, physical poise, energy, humor and compassion enable him to captivate all kinds of audiences.

I have personally had the delight of experiencing Michael's ability to deal with circumstances that are the standard nightmares for any communicator. In giant lecture halls, with a few minutes to go before commencement, the lights have gone out; audio-visual, sound systems and air conditioning have broken down; chairs and desks have collapsed under participants; firebells and bombscares have interrupted; last minute changes have been requested; coffee has been spilled on his lecture materials...

Not once did I see him falter. Not once did he fail to handle the situation with poise and humor, turning imminent disaster into inevitable success.

Indeed, when you read *Present Yourself!*, you will be reading a book, to recoin a familiar phrase, by a preacher who practices what he preaches about the practice of preaching!

In reading the book, you will actually feel as if you are part of one of the presentations for which the author is renowned.

My own international lecturing career was profoundly and positively affected by Michael, who helped me to apply to my own presentations many of the principles expressed in this book, particularly those that relate to his interpretation of the work of F. Mathias Alexander. Working with Michael has allowed me to communicate my thoughts more completely and effortlessly to my audiences.

One of the hallmarks of a commitment to excellence in any discipline is a never-ending search for accurate and objective feedback regarding one's performance. Over the twelve-year period that Michael and I have worked together, we have provided each other with critical information regarding our respective performances. Cooperating in this way, we have discovered insights that challenged us to discover new levels of presentational power. This approach to giving and receiving feedback—about which you will shortly be reading—is inspirational and invaluable.

When I first started my own research into the functioning of the human brain and subsequently developed Mind Mapping, I had a dream that others would have the same vision and translate it into different realities.

Present Yourself! is one of my dreams come true. With clarity, concision and veracity, Michael has accurately interpreted my own work and the work of others, such as Roger Sperry and F.M. Alexander, applying his own exceptional creativity to stamp a new coin.

Present Yourself! enables each one of us to gain access to our own rich resources and to express confidently and comprehensively the wealth and depth of our own unique knowledge, questionings, beliefs and enthusiasms.

This precious book is for the beginner and the advanced communicator; it is for trainers; for teachers; for managers; for anyone who has to speak in front of large groups; for anyone speaking to the smallest of groups.

It is for You.

It will become the standard work in its field.

Tony Buzan
Marlow, U.K.
September 1987

Introduction

Think about the last presentation you attended...

Was it fascinating? Engaging? Highly informative?

How much of it do you remember?

The average presentation is boring and easy to forget. Boring, because fear causes presenters to limit their natural expressiveness and seek refuge in mediocrity. Easy to forget, because presentations are usually designed and delivered in a fashion that ignores the most fundamental organ of human communication: the brain.

The human brain is the most magnificent instrument in the world, more complex and powerful than the greatest supercomputers. Yet, ninety-five percent of what we know about the brain has only been discovered in the last ten years.[1] We are just learning how to apply this knowledge to improving human memory, learning and communication.

We have discovered that our brains have evolved over millions of years to help us learn and effectively communicate with one another. And we know that every healthy baby is born with a tremendous capacity for vibrant and expressive communication. All too often, however, that natural capacity is stifled by a schooling process that encourages an exaggerated fear of making mistakes.

Freedom from fear and a practical understanding of the workings of the brain are essential ingredients for high performance presentations.

Present Yourself! goes right to the heart of these two issues.

In the chapters that follow, you'll learn about the brain's complexity and potential as the center of all communication and, thus, the key to presentation skills. We will consider the popular notion of left-brain/right-brain and its implications for giving well-organized, creative presentations.

You will be introduced to Mind Mapping—a revolutionary alternative to outlining, that gives you access to your brain's unlimited potential for creativity. This technique will help you generate ideas for your presentations faster and with greater flexibility. It will enhance your ability to organize and remember your material while encouraging more spontaneity and originality in your delivery.

You will also learn a number of simple, effective strategies for rehearsing and mastering your material, including how to program your brain for success every time you present by using positive visualization.

In addition to learning about the practical workings of your own brain, you will also gain major insights into the workings of the brains of your audience. We'll focus on how to think about them and anticipate their needs. This is simple common sense, the importance of which can't be overemphasized.

You will be given eight specific keys to making the content and timing of a presentation 'brain-friendly', and therefore engaging and unforgettable. You'll learn how to create a brain-nourishing environment, considering everything from lighting and ventilation to your appearance and audio-visual aids, and how each of these elements can have a profound effect on your audience's ability to understand and retain what you say.

Understanding your brain and the brains of your audience will build your confidence and make you a better speaker. Yet, in order to be a superior presenter—the best you can be—you must also learn to recognize and transform the energy of fear. Fear is a universal phenomenon experienced by every speaker. According to a recent poll, public speaking is the number one fear of almost half the population![2] Nearly everyone has experienced feelings of nervousness, stiffness and uncertainty while addressing a group. Fear often causes people to focus on *surviving* their presentations with a minimum of risk. As a result, they deliver unimaginative and mechanistic speeches, paralyzing their natural self-expression and anesthetizing their audiences.

This book is based on the ideas that everyone is capable of doing much more than merely surviving a presentation and that speaking to a group can be a scintillating, enjoyable and fulfilling experience.

Present Yourself! deals with the issue of fear head on. You will gain an understanding of the subtle mechanisms of fear, so that you can control your reaction to it before it interferes with your performance. You will learn how to take the energy that fear provides and turn it to your advantage. I will introduce you to powerful methods for developing fear-free, articulate body language, including a consideration of some of the trade secrets of the theatrical profession, all of which will greatly enhance the impact of every presentation you give.

The entire book is devoted to showing you how to enjoy being yourself in front of a group; how to make the most of all your abilities and natural expressiveness.

It is a common belief that people are either inherently comfortable and effective in front of groups or they're not. *Present Yourself!* is based on the conviction, born out of years of experience, that everyone is capable of learning how to give a *superior* presentation.

You already have every basic tool you need to become a superior presenter. This book is designed to help you make the most of those tools. You don't need to try to be something you are not. You don't need to be afraid...You don't need to be slick...You need only apply some simple, common sense and start presenting what you have to give— honestly, intelligently, sensitively and powerfully.

This is what *Present Yourself!* is all about.

In short, you'll see that becoming a better presenter is something that you have every capability of doing right now—if you are willing to take on the challenge of allowing yourself to do so.

Through my Washington, D.C.-based company, *High Performance Learning*, I've led seminars for people from all walks of life, from senior executives and other employees of IBM, DuPont, General Motors, AT&T and many other corporations, to the U.S. Army, the National Guard, school systems, government offices, police departments and hospitals. They have ranged from beginners or presentation-phobics to experienced trainers and top-level professional speakers.

The richest experience I have in my work is watching people—whatever their level—discover how enjoyable it is to stand in front of a group without fear, pretense or unnecessary effort and give the very best of themselves to an audience.

And then to hear them say, "Why didn't anyone ever tell me that this could be so much fun?"

As you read this book, I wish this joy to you.

> Michael J. Gelb
> Washington, D.C.
> March, 1988

CHAPTER 1

Meet Your Brain

An interest in the brain requires no justification other than a curiosity to know why we are here, what we are doing here, and where we are going.

Dr. Paul MacLean, Director
Laboratory of Brain Evolution
and Behavior, National Institute of Mental Health

Our educational system, and modern society generally, discriminate against one whole half of the brain. In our present educational system, the attention given to the right hemisphere is minimal, compared to the training lavished on the left side.

Roger Sperry, Nobel Laureate
in physiology and medicine

Your brain is a remarkable instrument. Right now, as you read this page, it is making 100,000 chemical reactions per second. Its 12 billion neurons have the potential to make more patterns of connection than the number of atoms estimated to exist in the universe. The neural circuitry of your brain is at least 1400 times more complex than the entire world telephone system.[1]

A great deal of evidence suggests that our brains store the memory of everything we've ever seen, heard, touched, smelled or thought. Its capacity appears to be unlimited.[2]

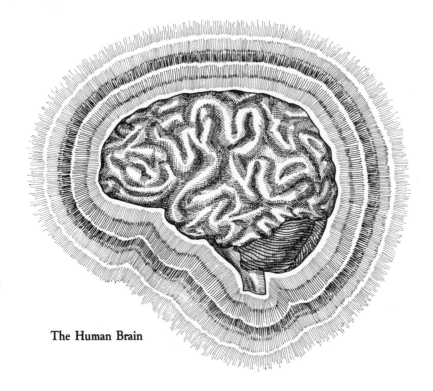

The Human Brain

This vast capacity, however, lies dormant because most of us have never learned how to fully access our brains. Psychologists estimate that we tap less than one percent of our brain's potential.[3]

Why? Most of us haven't 'met' our brains. In school, we're given courses in arithmetic, history and science—but aren't taught about the brain and its unlimited possibilities. One rarely comes to appreciate the brain's fundamental relationship to creativity, learning, memory and communication.

Or to making presentations.

All Presentations Are Brain-Based

Consider what happens during a presentation. A presenter's brain 'talks' to the brains of the audience members. Right now, for example, my brain is generating these words for your brain, through your eyes, to read. All communication is 'brain-to-brain' communication.

Yet, if you ever read a book or attended a course in presentation skills or public speaking, the brain probably wasn't mentioned. Whether you're a veteran presenter or a beginner, you've probably never prepared a presentation from a 'brain-based' perspective.

Without a brain-based perspective, you run the risk of using only half your brain and having only half the impact you could have on your audience. Let me explain.

'Left-Brain' Bias

In the early 1970s, Dr. Roger Sperry, a Nobel Laureate in physiology and medicine, did pioneering research leading to the popular notion of 'left-brain' and 'right-brain' thinking.

By studying the brain waves of people engaged in learning different kinds of tasks, Sperry and his colleagues concluded that each of the brain's two hemispheres—or sides—tend to specialize in certain kinds of thought. The left hemisphere was found to be primarily responsible for processing logic, language, details, mathematical reasoning and analysis, while the right side deals with rhythm, color, spatial relationships, imagination and synthesis.[4]

Unfortunately, our education grooms us from an early age to overemphasize 'left brain' activities.

Reading, writing and arithmetic—the three 'R's—are the first three subjects most of us study. Those who excel in these 'left-brain' dominant skills are considered class 'brains'—most likely to succeed.

The 'Logical' Brain Functions

On the other hand, children who excel in creative doodling, daydreaming and drumming innovative rhythms on their desks are viewed in a different light. These expressive, imaginative children are often labeled as 'behavioral problems'.

'Right-brain' characteristics such as daydreaming, imagination and humor are rarely encouraged in the process of schooling.

After school we enter the workplace, where organization and efficiency are often rewarded at the expense of imagination and creativity.

As a result, we may approach all our presentations with a limiting 'left-brain' bias.

The 'Imaginative' Brain Functions

Whole-Brained Presentations

Business people, teachers and others will usually assemble a factual presentation, offer it in a step-by-step, detail-oriented way, and assume it will be well-received.

While a presentation must be based on informative, well-organized material, it nevertheless needs other facets to be compelling—like variation in pacing, articulate body language and plenty of vivid verbal and visual imagery.

Why? Researchers have found that the brains of audience members tend to key on the body language, rhythm and imagery that speakers create more than on the words they say. These 'right hemisphere' elements are more engaging than the words themselves.[5]

So, to make sure your presentation is engaging and memorable, you must use your whole brain—integrating imagery and intuition with logic and analysis.

Summary

In order to give a powerful presentation, you must meet your brain—your whole brain. Only by using both its 'sides'—the logical and the imaginative—will you be able to communicate fully with the brains of your audience.

How can you start using both sides of your brain to make your presentations that effective?

In the next chapter, you will learn a whole-brain technique for generating and organizing ideas for your presentations.

You will be astonished at what your brain—the same one you've been carrying around with you all these years—can do.

CHAPTER 2

Map Your Mind

Mind Mapping is to the information and space ages as outlining was to the medieval and industrial ages.
Tony Buzan

Chris, a manager at a large corporation, regularly gives speeches and presentations. For many years he found this to be an almost unbearably difficult undertaking. His main problem was his difficulty with generating and organizing ideas. Although he was very knowledgable in his subject, he often found that when he sat down to prepare a speech, his mind would seem to go blank.

Chris, like most of us, was trained to generate and organize his thoughts using an outline. As we all know, an outline begins with the Roman numeral 'I'.

Chris would often sit at his desk for long periods of time waiting for Idea Number One. After what seemed like an eternity, he'd get his idea, and move on from there.

He would often find that when he got down to, say, 'III C', it should really be 'II A'. He'd start crossing out and drawing arrows and suddenly realize that his neat outline had become a mess. Sometimes at this point, he'd begin doodling or daydreaming; at other times, he'd just crumple his paper in frustration and start again. Over the years, he has filled many a wastebasket to overflowing.

Chris's Outline

The Trouble With Outlining

Chris is not alone. My research shows that the average executive spends the equivalent of three days preparing a forty-five minute presentation—a period full of frustration, discarded ideas and crumpled-up work sheets.

When we try to generate and organize thoughts for a presentation, we usually waste a lot of time and energy waiting for our good ideas to emerge.

The only tool we're ever taught to aid us in idea generation is the time-honored system of outlining. This method slows our thinking and limits our creativity.

Why? Because outlining imposes order *prematurely* on the process of thinking, thereby interfering with the speed and range of our idea generation. It is a lopsidedly 'left-brained' technique.

Our brains possess an unlimited potential for idea generation. They work best when we allow our ideas to flow freely *before* attempting to organize.

So, when we force a confining, half-brained system such as outlining on our flowing, active whole brain, we slow down its productivity, and all too often we wrench it to a halt. It then can't generate ideas effectively.

We also require a high degree of logical thinking in order to plan a compelling, organized sequence for our presentations. Without organization, creativity is stillborn.

Ideally, we need a hybrid alternative to outlining; a technique that is 'right-brain' oriented enough to help our minds create ideas freely, yet allows the 'left brain' to play its part in ensuring order and attention to detail.

Enter Mind Mapping.

Mind Mapping: An Introduction

Mind Mapping was developed in the early 1970s by British author and brain researcher Tony Buzan. Buzan developed it as a whole-brain alternative to outlining. Mind Mapping makes it easier to access your ideas while enhancing your ability to organize them. It allows the analytical, detail-oriented left side to work in harmony with the more imaginative right.[1]

A Mind Map is a simple, easy way to represent your ideas using key words, colors and imagery. Its non-linear format encourages you to begin generating ideas immediately and allows you to put a tremendous amount of significant information on one piece of paper.

There are seven guidelines to effective Mind Mapping. Before I take you through a simple exercise in Mind Mapping a presentation, let me introduce them to you.

1. Start your map by drawing a picture of your topic in the center of your paper. This drawing will serve as the 'home base' for your creative associations. Pictures help to 'jump-start' your right hemisphere. They are much easier to remember than words and, strange as it may seem, will enhance your ability to think creatively about your subject. Don't worry if you think you can't draw, just do the best you can. You will still get the 'brain benefits'—without being a Picasso.[2]

Central Image

2. Use key words. Key words are information rich. They are the 'nuggets' of recall and creative association. Research shows that key words can be generated faster than the sentences used in outlines, without sacrificing meaning.[3] Key words are also easier to remember than sentences.

Generating ideas in key word form is easy. For example, if you were giving a speech on the plays of Shakespeare, one of your key words might be 'Hamlet', which could then trigger 'second level' key words, such as 'Prince' or 'Denmark'. Examples of *non*-key words might be 'the' or 'and'.

Key Words

3. Connect the key words with lines radiating out from your central image. By linking words with lines, you'll show clearly how one key word relates to another. Connect the lines for maximum clarity.

4. Print your key words. The printed word is much easier to read and remember.

5. Print one key word per line. By doing this, you minimize clutter and leave yourself free to find the maximum number of creative associations for each word. Occasionally, you may feel compelled to print a phrase or sentence, but it's best to maintain the discipline of one word per line.

One Per Line

6. Use colors, pictures and codes for emphasis. These can be used to highlight important points and to show relationships between different branches of your map. You might, for instance, prioritize your main points through color-coding: highlighting in yellow your most important points, using blue for your secondary points, etc. Pictures and images should be used wherever possible as they stimulate your creative association and greatly enhance your memory. Codes, such as asterisks, exclamation points, letters and numbers, can be used to show relationships between concepts and as tools to further organize your map.

Colors, Pictures, Codes

7. Free-associate, then organize. The process of making a Mind Map to prepare a speech or presentation is divided into two major phases.

a) The first focuses on quickly generating as many ideas as possible. In this *free association phase*, you simply let your mind go and print as many key words and images as you possibly can. Even if a word seems ridiculous or irrelevant, put it down and keep the process flowing. In so doing, you'll be surprised to see how easy it is to get access to all that you know. You'll also enjoy discovering how seemingly-irrelevant associations can lead you to new creative insights.

b) After your brain has generated a wealth of associations, you'll enter into the second part of the process: *the organization phase*. In this phase, you'll examine your map from a more analytical perspective, eliminating elements that now seem superfluous, and consolidating your key concepts. Here you can use numbers, additional colors, letters or other codes to impose a clear sequence on your material. In some instances you may wish to redo your map in order to organize it further. If so, you might, for example, put your first point at one o'clock and proceed accordingly in a clockwise rotation. You can then, if you so desire, translate the map into outline form!

Mind Mapping Your Presentation

Mind Mapping is very easy. You don't need much to practice it—just your brain, a few colored pens, a piece of paper and a willingness to learn something new.

Try making a Mind Map to help you prepare for your next presentation. Or if you just want to experiment with Mind Mapping, make up a topic. Use the following instructions to guide you.

► To begin, get a large sheet of blank white paper—the bigger the better—and, ideally, five or more colored pens. You may also wish to use phosphorescent highlighters for extra color. (One pen and a small sheet of paper will still work in a pinch.) Place the paper horizontally on a desk in front of you.

► Having identified the topic for your presentation, draw a representative image in the middle of the paper. It doesn't matter if the image is abstract or concrete as long as it reminds you of your topic. Draw it as vividly as you can, using at least three different colors. Have fun, and don't worry about the accuracy of your drawing. (Remember guideline #1.)

► Now, look at your sketch and start printing key words on lines radiating out from your central image. Remember to print on the lines, one key word at a time, and keep the lines connected (guidelines #2–5). Use pictures and colors whenever possible (guideline #6). Let your associations occur spontaneously (guideline #7a), filling the page as quickly as you can. If you run out of room and the ideas are still flowing, get another piece of paper and keep going. If you get stuck, choose any key word on your map and immediately print your first association with that word—even if it seems ridiculous or irrelevant. Keep your associations flowing, and don't worry about making sure that every word is 'right'.

▶ When you feel you have generated enough material, take a look at the result: all the ideas for your presentation spread across one page. Having given your right brain the spotlight as the generator of these ideas, shift focus and use your left brain to put your map in order.

As you look at your map in this analytical way, you will begin to see relationships that will help you organize and integrate the presentation you are planning. Look for words that appear repeatedly throughout your Mind Map. They often suggest the major themes that integrate the different aspects of your talk.

Connect related parts of your map with arrows, more lines, codes and colors—whatever works best for you. Eliminate elements that seem extraneous. Pare your map down to just the ideas you need for what you're going to say. Then put them in sequence. If necessary, recopy the map to make it neater and easier to follow (guideline #7b).

The Advantages of Mind Mapping

As you experiment with Mind Mapping, its advantages in comparison to outlining will become increasingly obvious.

Mind Mapping gives you easier access to your brain's potential. It allows you to get started quickly and to generate more ideas in less time. Its free-ranging format—adding words to one branch of your map one moment, then skipping over to another branch the next—increases your chances of generating new ideas.

Mind Mapping activates your whole brain. It lets you develop a logical sequence and detailed organization of your material while encouraging imagination and spontaneity.

Mind Mapping allows you to represent a tremendous amount of information in a relatively small space. You can have all your notes for a presentation on one piece of paper, with your ideas arranged in a way that encourages you to see relationships between them. Mind Mapping gives you a clear view of *both the details and the whole picture* of your presentation.

Mind Mapping also makes memorizing your presentation much easier. Colors, images and key words, the three central ingredients of Mind Maps, are much more engaging to the brain than sentences. A well-made Mind Map is almost impossible to forget! (See Chapter 5 for information on using Mind Maps as a tool for memorizing your speech.)

Most importantly, Mind Mapping is more fun than outlining. It encourages creativity and humor in the process of developing a presentation, which in turn leads to a more lively and engaging delivery.

Summary

If you've done your first Mind Map as a result of reading this chapter, you now have a better idea of what your brain—your whole brain—can do.

Through Mind Mapping, you can start to infuse your presentations with more life, creativity and fun.

Yet, no matter how good you become at generating and organizing ideas, your presentation must be designed with the brains of your audience in mind. In the end, all that counts is what your audience gets.

In the next chapter, I'll discuss methods for ensuring that your audience gets your message.

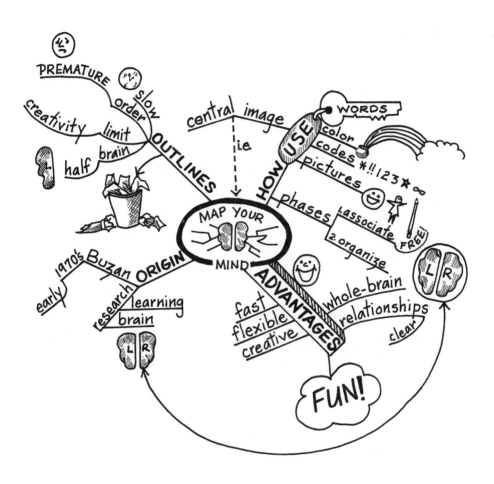

Chapter 2 Mind Map

CHAPTER 3

Think of Them

The meaning of a communication is the response that it elicits.
R. Bandler and J. Grinder,
authors of *Frogs into Princes*

A few years ago, I was scheduled to speak at a telephone company conference. The speaker who preceded me on the program was reputed to be one of the world's leading experts on the technology of communication. He gave what sounded like a tremendously authoritative speech, most of which was too technical for me to understand. As it turned out, most of the conference participants didn't understand it either.

Knowing something well and being able to communicate it effectively to an audience are two different things. Even an expert on the technology of communication is not necessarily an expert at communicating.

In order to give a powerful, effective presentation, it is essential to think about more than just yourself and your material—you must also consider your audience. Ultimately, the success of any presentation can only be measured from the audience's perspective. Although this is simple common sense, many of us get so caught up in our own material or nervousness that we forget to think about the audience. In other words, since all communication is 'brain-to-brain', we can't give effective presentations without focusing on the 'brains' of our audience members.

Many speakers make the mistake of assuming that their listeners will be like empty sponges, passively soaking up their remarks. Years of sitting in classrooms often conditions us to this standard of communication. It becomes all too easy to forget the audience and to have them forget you.

If you consider how you react when you are part of an audience, you will realize how much the success or failure of your presentation depends on taking your listeners' perspective into account.

It is essential to avoid allowing involvement with your material to overwhelm your awareness of the audience. Like the communications expert referred to earlier, many speakers become so enamored of their content they ignore their audience entirely.

Having extensive knowledge of a subject in no way ensures that you will be able to communicate it effectively. Your knowledge remains dormant unless your presentation is directed, from the beginning, to the brains of the audience.

The Audience As Empty Vessels

Know Your Audience

In order to know your audience, you *must* put yourself in their position. You will be better able to do this if you can answer the following questions about the composition, nature and mood of your audience:

► What is the audience expecting?

► What do they want to know?

► Are they attending voluntarily?

► How many people will be attending?

► What is the age and gender distribution of the group?

► What are their cultural/religious orientations?

► Do they speak a particular jargon?

► Are decision makers present? Who are they?

► What will the audience be feeling? Will they be energetic, enthusiastic, relaxed, tired, irritable or hostile?

► What activities will precede or follow the presentation—other presentations? Cocktails? Meals?

► To sum up, with what expectations or prejudices will their brains be filled as they prepare to listen to me?

By applying what you have learned from these questions to the design of your presentation, you will be much more likely to achieve a working rapport with the audience. Rapport provides the essential context for successful communication.

Intelligence Gathering

To answer the questions described above, take every opportunity to obtain information about the audience before you present. Here are some simple ways to gather this 'intelligence'.

Start by questioning whoever invited you to make your presentation. Many people are afraid that they will be perceived as nosey or rude for asking questions. On the contrary, experience shows that your thoroughness and interest will be appreciated.

Then, speak to anyone who is familiar with the group you will be addressing. It's especially valuable to interview speakers who have addressed your audience previously.

In the meantime, read anything that might give you useful information about your audience—such as annual reports, company publications or newspaper and magazine articles.

One of my favorite techniques for getting to know the audience is to arrive early and make informal contact with a few of the participants. I can often find out a great deal about the mood and expectations of the group by initiating friendly conversation. This allows me to dis- cover any potential problems and address the up-to-the-minute concerns of the audience. In one instance, twenty minutes before beginning a two-day seminar, I discovered through an informal conver- sation that one third of the participants had just been informed they might be laid off from their jobs. With the help of a quick Mind Map- ping session, I altered my design accordingly and made the most of a potentially disastrous situation.

Another time, I prepared a speech for a client I hadn't worked with in over seven years. The speech was to be given at the end of a conference to 500 senior managers from around the world. I was not able to get a clear idea of how to focus my speech from discussions with the people who invited me, and other sources were not readily available. I planned my speech based on what I knew about the group seven years ago, but decided to travel to the conference site the evening before in order to gather 'intelligence' from participants. I discovered that the group had changed dramatically, and realized that the focus of my speech was inappropriate. I altered my design and began by talking about the changes I'd observed. The audience knew immediately that I was speaking *to them*, and this rapport created the context for success.

Whether you are leading a seminar, addressing a group of 500 or talking to your local PTA, it is critically important to know your audience and to *think of them*.

Set Your Objectives

Having thoroughly considered your audience, you must decide what you want them to *know* and to *do* as a result of your presentation.

Carefully setting your objectives is a matter of common sense, yet it is amazing to discover how rarely it is practiced. All too often, presentations are approached with fuzzy intentions. Failure to set clear objectives is a hallmark of mediocrity; choosing your objectives consciously, therefore, is a critical key to high performance.

Start by generating your objectives through Mind Mapping.

Then, write them down in complete sentences as this will enable you to further hone your objectives. For example, if you are giving a sales presentation, you might write the following: "At the end of this presentation, my audience will know the three major reasons why my product is superior to the competition's, and they will buy it."

Or, if you're a teacher giving a lecture, you might write this: "All my students will leave this lecture knowing the seven major reasons for the French Revolution so that they will be able to use that information to excel on next week's test."

To better focus your objectives, try the following approach: Imagine each member of the audience being interviewed by the national news media immediately after your presentation. Envision them being asked,

It's what your audience gets...

"What did you learn in this presentation?" and "What will you do differently as a result of this presentation?" Further, imagine them answering confidently in terms of your objectives for them. By focusing your objectives in this way, you will be clarifying what will be communicated brain-to-brain, thereby sharpening your impact.

Summary

In this chapter, I've emphasized the importance of knowing your audience and applying this knowledge in every presentation. I've also highlighted the necessity of setting specific objectives for every presentation you give—objectives that take into account what you want your audience to *know* and *do* as a result of your presentation.

Always remember that the success of your presentation is ultimately measured in terms of what the audience receives. *It's what your audience gets that counts.*

In the next chapter, I'll take this idea a step further by showing you how an audience remembers. Through developing a deeper understanding of the brains of your audience, you can virtually guarantee that they will remember everything you wish.

Chapter 3 Mind Map

CHAPTER 4

Build Their Recall

Understanding is not the same as remembering.
Tony Buzan

If you are engaged in preparing a presentation in the manner I have been suggesting, you may be feeling a certain excitement—a sense that already your presentation is going to be far better than any you've ever given.

It will be!

Yet, in order for it to be truly successful, you must make sure that your audience *remembers* it.

Before you continue, please try the following simple exercise. Below are forty words. Read through them one time only—left to right. Don't study them. Read each word to yourself, taking no more than sixty seconds to read them all.

Forty-Word Memory Exercise

car   deck   table   tree   snow   bottle money   dog
pole   sand   sky   dog   plant   book   soap   spoon   music
plant   rug   Groucho Marx   plant   cellar gate   pillow dog
presentation skills trunk   paper   road   knife   stool   hay
smile   string plant   wheel   air   expert rain   bird

Make a note of the words you remember, and ask yourself why you remembered those particular words.

This exercise highlights the way in which memory works during a period of learning. Most people are more likely to remember the *first* few words on the list—car, deck, table—and the *last* few words on the list—air, expert, bird—than the words in the middle. Exceptions include words that are *repeated*—plant and dog—words that are *unusual*—Groucho Marx—or those with special personal meaning in their context—presentation skills.

Your Audience's Memory

Along the same lines, studies show that when people attend a presentation, they recall certain key parts of it more vividly than others.[1]

Specifically, their brains lock onto a presentation's *beginning* (the primacy effect) and *end* (the recency effect) and any of its elements that are *unusual*, *repeated* over and over, or *personally involving*.

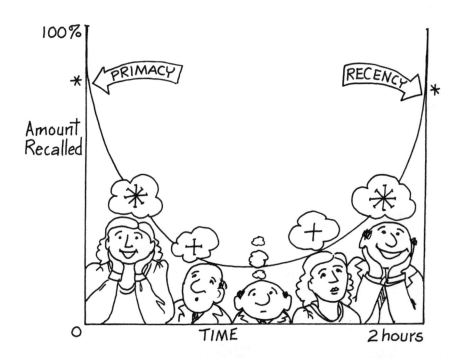

How can you help your audience remember your presentation? Simple: by applying an understanding of how recall functions over time to the design and delivery of your material.

The Five Keys to Audience Recall

If you want your presentation to be memorable, you must keep the following five points in mind as you develop and deliver your presentation: *Begin powerfully.* Emphasize your main points in the beginning of your talk. *Repeat regularly.* Review your key points throughout. *Emphasize unusually.* Make your key points in humorous, outstanding or unusual ways. *Maximize involvement.* Create plenty of opportunities for the audience to get involved with your presentation. *End powerfully.* Emphasize your main points again at the end—finish with a bang!

Now, let's go into each of these ideas in more detail:

Begin powerfully. There are two major components necessary for taking advantage of the primacy effect.

Make contact. Start by making contact with your audience while focusing on your objectives. The best way to do this is to zero in on what you want your audience to get from the presentation. *Wanting to communicate* with your audience is the key to making contact with them. This attitude will come through in your eyes, your posture and in the way you move. It is more important than any icebreaking gimmick. Having said that, there are a number of useful ways to get things rolling. You can begin by asking your audience a question, real or rhetorical; you can tell a joke or a story; initiate a discussion; offer an exercise or a challenge; use audio-visuals; even act out a skit.

I recommend that you avoid using any kind of 'canned' opening. Use your creativity to make up your own. Whatever technique you use to break the ice, make sure that it is related to what you want the audience to remember. For example, if I were giving a presentation on

"Making Your Presentations Unforgettable," I might use the forty-word memory test as an icebreaker.

Give the audience an overview. Research shows that an audience responds positively to being given a sense of the 'shape' of a presentation.[3] The preacher's proverbial advice of "tell 'em what you're gonna tell 'em" is sound. Let the people know where you are taking them and how you are going to get them there. For example, in my speech on "Making Your Presentations Unforgettable," I might follow my forty-word icebreaker exercise by saying something like: "In the next hour, I'm going to show you how to make your presentations unforgettable, every time. The key to giving memorable presentations lies in understanding how an audience's memory works. Before you leave here today, you will know the five crucial elements that make a presentation unforgettable. These five elements are. . ."

Repeat regularly. Just as you were more likely to remember the words 'plant' and 'dog' in the forty-word exercise, so your audience will be better able to remember points that you repeat regularly. Commercial advertisers often follow this principle—and all the other principles outlined in this chapter—to the extreme by incessantly repeating product names or telephone numbers ("Call 979-9000, that's 979-9000; remember, call 979-9000. . .").

I'm not suggesting that you be extreme; only effective—in the manner, for example, of one of my favorite speakers of all time: Dr. Martin Luther King, Jr. He drilled a powerful idea into a nation's consciousness by repeating rhythmically, "I have a dream."

Emphasize unusually. Emphasize your key points by making them in unusual, outstanding ways. The brains of the audience seek stimulation and entertainment. As such, make your key points in an exceptional, outstanding or humorous way, and the audience will eagerly grasp and remember them.

A classic example of the power of this idea was provided some years ago by Nikita Khruschev, then the Premier of the Soviet Union. While delivering a speech at the United Nations, he punctuated his statement,

"We will bury you" (directed at the United States), by pounding a shoe on the podium. The next day, newspaper headlines around the world read: "We Will Bury You," and featured extensive passages from his speech.

In fact, Khruschev had both his shoes on at the time. His was not the act of a madman. He had borrowed an aide's shoe to make his point unforgettable.

The idea is not to be dramatic or funny solely for the sake of being dramatic or funny, but to ensure, through your novelty, that your key points are remembered. For example, one of the most effective presentations I've ever heard about was given at a large chemical company. When a chemist there wanted to emphasize for his audience how nontoxic a new chemical product was, he simply picked up a spoon and started eating some of it right in the middle of his presentation. This was so extraordinary that people there still talk about it—and the point he made—ten years later.

You don't have to bang your shoe or eat chemicals to make a point, but if you want your audience to remember your message, you must find a way within the context of your own 'comfort zone' to express your points powerfully.

You can use posture, gestures, eye contact and voice to power home your message (see Chapter 8: *Let Your Body Talk*). You can also use colorful audio-visuals, stories, skits, jokes, parables—anything that captures your audience's attention *as long as it's related to your subject*.

And bearing in mind the points made in Chapter 2: *Meet Your Brain*, the elements of humor, drama and color will help you to engage the 'whole brain' of your audience.

Maximize involvement. In order to maximize your own involvement, you may choose to take a piece of paper and make a Mind Map of all possible ways you can involve the audience in your presentation.

If your audience can develop a sense of personal association with your presentation—through discussion, exercises, questions (real or rhetorical)—they'll remember it more vividly. Did you know that asking an audience a rhetorical question significantly raises their attention level?[4]

Furthermore, if you can structure your presentation so that the audience is able to discover the key points for themselves, they'll feel even more involved, and their recall will be even greater. Remember that the root of the word 'education' is *'educare'*, meaning 'to draw out'—not to 'stuff in'! Therefore, *'educare'* your audience whenever possible.

I often view a presentation as an opportunity to create a context in which my audience can discover for themselves the things I've come to present to them. My role is to facilitate that process, to validate and elaborate on their discoveries.

In addition to structuring your presentation as described above, you can also maximize audience involvement by "speaking the language that your audience speaks." You'll be best able to do this if you follow the principles of audience 'intelligence gathering' discussed in Chapter 3: *Think of Them.*

One of the great examples of the effectiveness of this approach was provided by John F. Kennedy in his famous speech at the Berlin Wall. Kennedy began his speech with a few simple words in German: "Ich bin ein Berliner" (I am a Berliner). He practiced those words for weeks before his trip and won the hearts of his listeners by speaking their language, literally and figuratively. (It's also interesting to note that Kennedy used this phrase to start his speech, thereby applying the principles of *beginning powerfully* and *maximizing involvement.*)

End powerfully. Think of the best play you have ever seen, the best movie, the greatest concert, the finest novel you've ever read. How did it end? Powerfully. Clearly.

An audience's recall is always high at the end of a presentation, even if they don't know the end is coming. In order to take full advantage of this recency effect, it is essential to emphasize your main points again just before you close. You have set objectives for what you want your audience to know and to do; *this is your last chance to make sure that they know it and do it.* Again, the preacher's advice is sound, "Tell 'em what you told 'em." Give a clear review of the points you've made (if you used a graphic for your overview, you can use it again here) and, if appropriate, issue a call to action (tell them what you want them to do). Your presentation will end powerfully and clearly—with a bang!

Vital Information: Timing and Breaks

There are three more vital applications of the information on audience recall: start on time, give appropriate breaks and finish on time. These may seem obvious, yet experience shows that they are often abused. As they are essential ingredients for a high performance presentation, let's look at each one in more depth.

Be prepared to start on time. As we have seen, first impressions are very powerful. If you aren't prepared to start on time, you will be coming up to the plate with two strikes against you. Lateness is the ultimate negative primacy. You must always be ready to start on time.

The truth is, most presentations don't begin on time because organizations tend to tolerate lateness. You, however, must never be the reason for the delay. It's also important to remember that because of this lateness phenomenon, you will probably have fewer minutes to deliver your material than you expected. Plan accordingly.

Give your audience, and yourself, a break. Over the past ten years, I have given thousands of presentations, lasting anywhere from twenty minutes to five days. At the end of these sessions, participants regularly comment that not only did they learn more than they usually do in the same amount of time, but they came away with more energy than when they started. More than anything else, I attribute these good results to the fact that I always give my audience, and myself, regular breaks. And, I give these breaks *before* they are desperately needed.

Remember the recency effect: recall rises for the last part of a session. All too often, presentations drag on for 75, 90, even 120 minutes or longer. In these cases, the audience is usually shifting, itching and scratching, desperate for a break. When the break is finally called, people dash for the door—the recency effect being "Let me out of here!"

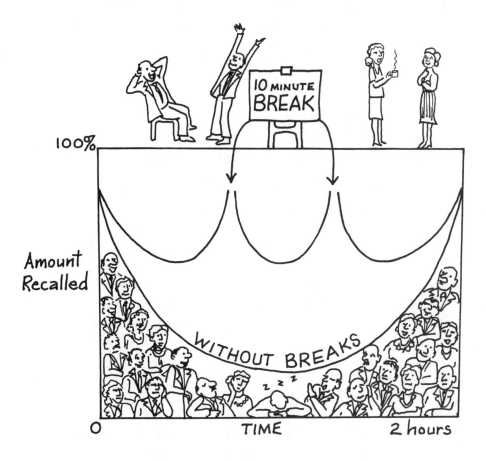

The Ten-Minute Break

Presenters who abuse their audience in this manner will often say that they are reluctant to give breaks because "it's so difficult to get the audience back" (of course the audience doesn't want to come back, because they never know when they're going to get a break again!), and thus a vicious cycle is perpetuated.

Give your audience a break before they get desperate, preferably at a high point so they can return even more energized. Leave them with the positive recency effect of "What's next?!" instead of "Let me out of here!"

Breaks are therefore important not only as a means of regulating your audience's energy and attention; they are also essential for ensuring maximum recall. Research shows overwhelmingly that beyond fifty minutes, audience recall falls sharply. It declines at this point even if the audience's *understanding* remains high, because understanding is not the same as remembering.[5]

Research also shows that a ten-minute break, given at the end of a fifty-minute lecture, will improve the audience's recall of the material.[6] Appropriate breaks allow the brain to process and integrate the material it is receiving. Depending upon the time of day and the difficulty of the material, I give breaks every thirty to sixty minutes—from thirty-second stretch breaks to ten-minute leave-the-room breaks.

A useful guideline for longer presentations is ten minutes of break time per hour. I recommend that you resist the temptation to go on beyond sixty minutes, even if everything seems to be flowing nicely. Giving appropriate breaks is ultimately an art, based on developing sensitivity to your audience. The critical point is that breaks are an essential part of your presentation.

Since most presentations require an audience to remain in a focused mode of attention, the break should allow them to shift into a more relaxed state. You might, for example, encourage your audience to stretch, take a walk, and, if possible, get some fresh air. It's also a good idea to play music during the breaks. These activities change the pace, and will energize and refresh both you and your audience.

By giving your audience regular breaks, you will create more opportunities for powerful primacy and recency; everything you say will be more outstanding and therefore more memorable.

Finish on time. Never continue over your allotted time. There is no surer way to spoil an otherwise successful presentation. Even if you feel that your audience would like you to continue, don't. Resist the temptation. Let them ask you questions afterwards, if necessary. It is always better to leave them wanting more.

Before you begin speaking, jot down the time you are supposed to finish. Treat your finishing time as a contract made with your audience and arrange to have a clock in view to help you fulfill your commitment.

Summary

Can you remember the five principles of audience recall without looking back at the text? How about the three essential timing points? This information is so important that I urge you to commit it to memory. If you can consistently begin powerfully, repeat regularly, emphasize unusually, maximize involvement, and end powerfully, while giving appropriate breaks and starting and finishing on time, you will be able to guarantee an unforgettable presentation.

In this chapter, we have emphasized the keys to building your audience's recall. In the next chapter, we are going to focus on how you can build your own recall so that you remember your material effortlessly and present it masterfully.

Chapter 4 Mind Map

CHAPTER 5

Perfect Practice

Practice doesn't make perfect. Perfect practice makes perfect.
Vince Lombardi

In order to give a masterful presentation, you must be able to remember what you want to say.

Rehearsal is the key to mastery.

Actors, musicians and athletes all rehearse regularly. They are immersed in demanding activities full of fine points—and they know rehearsing is essential to high performance. In the first four chapters of *Present Yourself!*, we've seen that giving high performance presentations is an equally demanding process. It is essential, therefore, to rehearse your presentations. Furthermore, the quality of your rehearsal must be up to a certain standard if it is to bring you maximum value.

Practicing Perfectly

How can you rehearse effectively, tuning your brain for high performance?

Most importantly, you should begin filling your brain with positive thoughts about your presentation right from the start.

When asked to do a presentation, many people will begin—consciously or unconsciously—to think negatively. In a word, they'll worry. And in worrying, they'll program their brains for failure.

Instead, program your brain for success. For example, from the first moment you find that you have to do a presentation, begin visualizing yourself delivering it masterfully. Visualize, as clearly as you can, the place where the presentation will be given. Imagine yourself feeling relaxed, confident, calm and poised. View yourself moving, gesturing and speaking in an easy, fluid manner. Finally, create an image of your audience engaged by, and involved in, your presentation.

Keep building these positive images—right through your actual presentation.

Positive, conscious visualization is one of the inner secrets of master performers in a wide range of disciplines. Athletes, actors, singers, musicians, dancers and speakers all use this powerful technique.

Your thoughts have an immediate and profound effect on the distribution of your muscle tone and the ability of your nerve impulses to fire in harmony. Research has shown that 'nourishing' your brain with positive images helps your nervous system to function at its peak. When positive visualization is practiced regularly, it can significantly enhance your performance.[1]

Making Visualization Work for You

You can visualize successfully. In order to develop confidence in your ability to create images, start by asking yourself whether you can describe the following: a tennis ball, an ice cream cone, a tiger, a beautiful beach, yourself. You obviously can. These images reside in the occipital lobe of your brain, which stores billions of images from your own personal history. This part of your brain has the potential, at this very moment, to store an infinite series of new images and to create an infinite number more.

Five keys to make visualization work for you are: study models of excellence; relax; use multisensory imagination; keep the visualization positive; and practice. Let's look at how these keys apply to preparing for a presentation.

Study models of excellence. In order to gain rich material for your conscious visualization, you may find it useful to identify presenters whom you consider to be models of excellence and study them. Some of my favorites include Martin Luther King, Jr., Winston Churchill and Muhammad Ali in his prime. Find your own examples of excellence and take every opportunity to learn from them.

Relax. Research shows that visualization exercises are more effective when practiced in a relaxed state.[2] Relaxing allows your visualization to have a deeper impact. You can precede your visualization practice with a short relaxation exercise,[3] or practice visualizing as you are waking or dozing off to sleep, as I do.

Use multisensory images. Use all your senses when imagining your excellent presentation. Imagine the feeling of your feet on the floor, your vision of the audience, the sounds in the room. The more vivid your imagination, the more powerful the result.

Keep your visualization positive. Imagine yourself calm and confident, poised and powerful, flowing effortlessly through your material. Think of yourself as an excellent presenter committed to getting better and better. Research suggests that positive visualization is effective because our thoughts have the power to energize the neuro-muscular mechanisms that will perform the action.[4] When you visualize yourself doing something well, you are programming your brain for success.

Practice. Reinforce your visualization of excellence regularly. By refining your visualization, you'll get better and better all the time.

Of course, visualization is most effective when combined with more traditional forms of practice. And your practice will be more effective if you can remember all your material. Before giving an overview of some simple rehearsal techniques, I'd like to introduce you to a very effective way to remember the material for your presentations.

The Mind Map Memory Method

Although it's fine to bring notes with you when you present, it's best to emancipate yourself from dependence upon them. You will always be

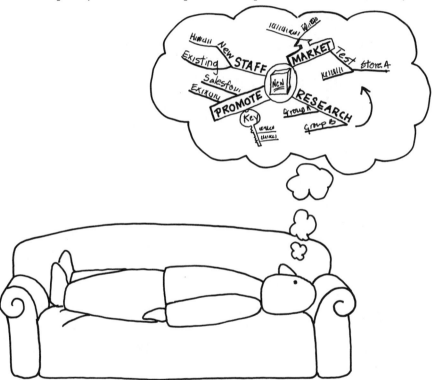

better able to present yourself if you work from memory. If you have used a Mind Map to prepare your presentation, you are already one step ahead.

Imagery, color and key words make Mind Maps easy to remember, and with a little practice you will find them almost impossible to forget. Start, of course, by making a clear, comprehensive and vivid Mind Map. Then, in order to make sure that you remember it, take out a new sheet of paper and re-create the map from memory. When you've fin-ished, check against the original map and fill in anything you may have left out. You will find that if you follow this re-creation process two or three times, the material will be almost unforgettable. To enhance your memory further, attach the map on a wall, close your eyes and practice re-creating it in your mind's eye. Open your eyes and check against the original. Do this until you can re-create the entire map effortlessly. Two or three times should be sufficient.

Strategies for Rehearsal

In addition to the Mind Map Memory Method, there are a number of other valuable rehearsal strategies—all of which will help you perform at your best. Experiment with the following, using those that work best for you.

▶ Deliver your presentation to yourself aloud. Become accustomed to the rhythm, timing and feel of your message.

▶ Tape record your presentation. Play the tape, listening to the quality of your voice and the overall coherence and flow of the presen-tation.

▶ Videotape your presentation. Play the tape and observe the way your posture and gestures relate to your message, again giving spe-cial attention to the overall coherence and flow of the presentation.

▶ Give your presentation to a friend or colleague. Do this first with-out asking for any feedback so you can get comfortable; then ask for constructive criticism.

▶ For particularly important presentations, bring together as many supportive friends or colleagues as you can and deliver your presen-tation to them. Ask them to play the role of the most critical, dis-ruptive audience they can imagine, to be 'devil's advocates', and to point out any possible weaknesses in your material or delivery.

Although this experience may be somewhat unsettling, it will prepare you ably for your actual presentation—which should seem relaxing by comparison.

► Time your practice sessions. Become familiar with the amount of time it takes to cover your key points. And bear in mind that your actual presentation will probably take longer than it does in rehearsal. Set minimum and maximum times for each 'branch' of your presentation. Anticipate the effect of questions and interruptions on your timing, and always have more material available than you will actually need.

► Practice with any audio-visuals or props you intend to use. Become fluent in any medium you intend to employ. (See Chapter 6 for more detailed advice.)

I recommend that you experiment with all of the above strategies, find the rehearsal methods that work best for you, and practice them faithfully.

Summary

The most important point of this chapter is to approach your presentation with a *positive attitude from the first moment*. You can develop this by applying the technique of visualization. The keys to imaging effectively are studying models of excellence; relaxing; using multisensory imagining; keeping the images positive; and practicing!

To memorize your material, apply the Mind Map Memory Method. Recreate your Mind Map, first on paper and then in your mind's eye. To rehearse further, practice aloud by yourself or with a friend. Use a tape recorder or video, or have a 'Devil's advocate' session. Make sure that you have mastered your audio-visuals and props, and that you have timed your presentation.

The techniques discussed in this chapter will help you to set the stage for high performance. In the next chapter, we'll look at how you can literally set the stage—the actual physical environment (lighting, ventilation, acoustics and a host of other factors)—in order to further guarantee your success.

Chapter 5 Mind Map

CHAPTER 6

Set Your Stage

The medium is the message.
Marshall McLuhan

The environment in which you give a presentation has many subtle but powerful effects. The lighting, air quality, even the shape of the room, along with many other factors including your appearance and audio-visuals, can have a profound influence on your audience's ability to enjoy and remember your presentation.

While a carefully constructed environment can enhance the effectiveness of your presentation, the usual environment in which presentations take place tends to distract from, or vitiate, your efforts to communicate. For example, the average presentation takes place under fluorescent lights. Considerable evidence suggests that fluorescent lighting discoordinates the two hemispheres of the brain, thereby interfering with an audience's ability to absorb information.[1] Moreover, when people are uncomfortable—perhaps because their chairs are constricting or the room in which they're seated is too hot—their attention level and ability to recall will suffer.

With these points in mind, take an active interest in 'setting the stage' before a presentation, and, whenever possible, shape the circumstances in order to create the ideal learning environment for your audience. This will require extra preparation, but I promise that your efforts will prove worthwhile.

Environmental Factors

The main factors to consider when setting your stage are:

Room and furniture. Always aim to give your presentation in a room that provides ample space for every member of your audience. Set up the chairs—and tables if necessary—in an arrangement most suited to the kind of presentation you are giving. For small groups of about twenty-five people or less, I find that a 'U' shape design is the most effective as it encourages maximum interaction and participation. For larger groups, I prefer a modified classroom style arrangement.

'U' Shape

Classroom Style

Whatever seating arrangement you use, it's a good idea to remove empty chairs from the room, or at least move them to one side. Vacant seats form a center of 'dead energy', which can unconsciously draw the audience's attention away from your message.

The important point is to set up your room and furniture in a manner that reflects concern about your audience. Consideration of this level of detail is a hallmark of excellence.

Decor. An audience seeks stimulation and involvement with its immediate surroundings. Many presentations are given in drab, generic rooms. Dull environments tend to have a dulling effect on the minds of an audience. Create an attractive, brain-nourishing environment. Fresh flowers, green plants and colorful visual aids enliven and engage your audience, thus making them more receptive to your message.

Lighting. Lighting is another important factor in a brain-nourishing environment. Unfortunately, the form of lighting available at most presentation sites—fluorescent lights—is mental junk food. In addition to their disorienting effect on the brain, fluorescent lights do not cast shadows very well, thereby interfering with the contrast necessary for clearer vision. They also often produce a low-level buzzing noise. These effects can distract your audience, who need to see and hear you clearly in order for your remarks to have full impact. Whenever possible, make your presentations in rooms with natural or incandescent lighting.

Air and temperature. Most presentations are given in rooms with poor ventilation and temperature control. Stuffy air can lull your audience into a sleepy state, and an uncomfortable room temperature is a constant distraction. Ideally, give your presentation in a well-ventilated room, with a temperature of between 65° and 68°.[2] You can often manage the air quality and temperature through the judicious opening and closing of doors and windows. If ideal temperatures cannot be met, it's better to err on the side of being too cool.

I also recommend that you maintain the quality of air in the room by asking your audience to refrain from smoking. Fresh air is already at a premium in most indoor environments. It is best to insist that your audience only smoke outside the room during the frequent breaks you'll be giving them. It's also a good idea to place five or six large green plants in the room. In addition to enlivening the environment, plants also help to freshen the air.

Your appearance. Preparing your appearance is another integral aspect of setting your stage. Audiences invariably react strongly to every facet of your appearance. A dragging shirt tail, mismatched colors and ill-fitting garments will all be distracting to your audience. Even the slightest quirk in your appearance is magnified in their eyes. So dress and groom yourself immaculately.

I refrain from giving more specific advice on how to dress because I want to encourage you in your own personal style. I will recommend, however, that you be better dressed than your audience, especially when presenting to people senior to you. Wear clothes that fit you well and allow for comfort and easy movement. Find a couple of outfits that look and feel great. If possible, wear them just for presentations. Enjoy looking your best, and let your clothes become part of your 'visualization of excellence'.

Your appearance will be affected by the extent to which you have rested and exercised, and also by your diet. If you are a professional presenter, or aim to be, I recommend that you condition yourself in a manner similar to that of a professional dancer or athlete. Your general fitness, exuberance and the sparkle in your eyes are the most important aspects of your appearance.

Your introduction. This is a key aspect in setting the stage for your presentation. It should affirm your credibility as a speaker and raise the energy and attention level of your audience. People often arrive at a presentation with their minds on the situations they've just left—from household problems to traffic jams; an effective introduction psychologically 'brings' them into the room.

Arrange to have the best speaker available introduce you. Be prepared with a Mind Map—or outline—of what you'd like this person to say. Ask the speaker to keep the introduction under two minutes, the objective being to create an environment of expectation and interest. Be certain that all questions concerning the availability of toilets, telephones, refreshments and other basic needs are answered before the formal introduction begins.

Audio-visual Aids

Audio-visual aids can play a powerful role in enhancing the impact and memorability of your presentation. When used properly, they can entertain and enliven your audience while increasing their receptivity and recall.

The proper use of audio-visual equipment requires keeping in mind a few simple points.

▶ Remember that the primary reason for using audio-visuals is to *highlight and emphasize the key points of your presentation*. Whether you're using a flipchart, overhead projector or any other medium, do not try to fill it with detailed information. Your audience will almost always be unable to follow information presented in this way. Many presenters, instead of using a picture to represent a thousand words, like to show pictures—or slides and flipcharts—of a thousand words. Use your audio-visuals to display images, key words or phrases that summarize and highlight your main points. They will be much more effective as brain stimuli for your audience.

▶ Don't rely on audio-visual aids to do your work for you. *You* must be the primary medium for delivering your information. Avoid hiding behind the audio-visuals or speaking to them. Your job is not to disappear in the dark while the audience looks at slides, or to talk to your flipchart. If you do, you'll lose your rapport with your audience—and the impact of your presentation will suffer.

► Only employ audio-visuals when needed. Used consciously, they are powerful tools for capturing the attention of an audience. *Be certain that your audience is seeing only what you want them to see and when you want them to see it.*

► If you plan to use complex audio-visual equipment, practice with it beforehand and learn its operational ins and outs thoroughly. Nothing will be more distracting to an audience, or potentially damaging to the impact of your presentation, than fumbling with your equipment onstage. Always be prepared for the possibility that your equipment will fail or that materials you requested will not be delivered.

► All visual materials should be *simple, clear and easy to see* from all parts of the room.

Let's consider how to make the most of some commonly used visual aids.

Flipcharts. Flipcharts are readily available, portable and easy to use. To make the most of this medium you must print legibly in large, bold letters, using different colors. Employ key words or phrases rather than sentences. Flipcharts are good for drawing diagrams, graphs and other pictures to illustrate your key points. Chart sheets should be uncluttered and easy to read. When appropriate, prepare your flipchart before your presentation, writing on every third sheet to prevent the audience from reading through the partially transparent paper.

A flipchart should only be used in a relatively small group. Sit at the back of the room before you begin your presentation to test its readability. Flipchart sheets can be awkward to turn, making it difficult to refer to previous sheets. You can partially overcome this by using multiple charts.

Overhead projectors. Overhead projectors allow you to present a great deal of vivid, visual information. They are much easier to see than flipcharts—because the projected image is illuminated and much larger—and can be used with groups of any size. This is a dynamic medium, which allows you to write easily while speaking. And because you face your audience while using an overhead, it's easy to maintain contact.

I recommend that you use single sheet transparencies because they allow you to refer quickly to previous material. Overhead projector pens come in a wide array of colors, making it easier to draw memorable images. When using the overhead for longer presentations, place it on a low table so that you can sit comfortably while drawing.

Projector bulbs have a tendency to burn out at awkward moments. Always come prepared with a spare bulb (or a backup machine). Check the focus before you begin, and regularly monitor the image on the screen to be sure that it remains centered and clear.

Slide projectors. Slides can add tremendous visual clarity, impact and entertainment. If you plan to use slides as part of your presentation, remember these few simple points: Think carefully about how each slide supports your objectives, showing the minimum number of slides necessary to illuminate each of your points. Too many slides can overload and exhaust your audience while obscuring your message. And leaving the lights off for extended periods will often result in loss of contact with your audience.

Use a high quality *autofocus* projector with a remote control device (or a projectionist), allowing you to move freely and interact with your audience. Always triple check to be sure that the slides are upright and in order.

Video and film. These can be the most engaging and entertaining audio-visual tools. They are so powerful, however, that they can often obscure the role of the presenter. Video and film *are* the presentation, best used as a substitute for a standup presentation rather than as a complement to it. So when using these media, bear in mind that you are functioning primarily as a facilitator and discussion leader.

A Few Other Points To Consider. . .

Handouts. Handouts can be an effective way for you to provide more detailed information to your audience. Distribute them at the end of your presentation or at a point when you will specifically refer to them; always direct your audience to a particular portion of the handout, giving them time to read it. When finished, ask the audience to put it aside.

Avoid telling your audience that you will be distributing handouts at the end of your session as this will often lead them to not pay attention. If you distribute the handout at the beginning of the presentation, your audience will tend to focus more on the handout than on what you have to say.

Music. It may have never occurred to you to add music to your presentation, but it is excellent brain food for your audience. Studies show that certain types of classical music—including the non-choral works of Beethoven, Mozart, Vivaldi and Bach—facilitate coherence between the right and left side of a listener's brain.[3] You may play this kind of music while your audience enters the room, during breaks, or as they are leaving. Using music in this way will heighten your audience's energy and receptivity while creating an aura of excellence.

Microphone. Only use a microphone when necessary. Amplified sound is often distorted and difficult to modulate properly.

When you have to use a microphone, the most important point is becoming comfortable with the amplified sound of your own voice. Always test the microphone before you begin speaking; and if you are inexperienced, take some extra time to practice. When using a standard microphone, aim it at your mouth from a constant distance of between six to eight inches away. Whenever possible, use a cordless collar microphone to allow maximum freedom of movement and more consistent voice modulation.

Mind Maps. You can greatly enhance the effectiveness of your presentations by using Mind Maps to communicate with your audience. Mind Mapping allows you to convey a great deal of information in a brain-compatible manner. Using Mind Maps successfully requires that you begin by giving a brief introduction of the technique. I usually tell my groups that "I am going to make a simple, easy map of the ideas I will be discussing." Then, as I am speaking, I use an overhead projector and colored pens to build a map of all my key points. As the map grows before their eyes, it creates an element of suspense that captures the audience's imagination. In addition to being easily memorable and information rich, this technique encourages high levels of attention and interest.

What If 'They' Won't Let Me Do It?

In making the above recommendations, I occasionally meet the objection, "They won't let us do this" or "It's just not possible in the place I work." Although there are occasions in which it is difficult to manipulate the environment in the manner suggested here, you will be surprised at what can be accomplished if you are insistent. Whether you are giving a presentation within your own organization or coming in from the outside, you can almost always create better conditions. Ultimately, everyone will be glad that you did.

I recommend creating your own environmental checklist for presentations and sending it, well in advance, to the logistics coordinator. Follow up with a phone call and review each item. Arrive early enough to check the details and make any last minute changes.

There will, of course, be times when your opportunity to create the environment is limited, such as when you follow other speakers at a conference. Nevertheless, you can still set your stage, even if it means simply rearranging a table at the front of the room, bringing your own flowers, or asking that empty chairs be removed before you begin. This action shows that you care. It is a display of your self-confidence and makes it clear that you are taking command.

Summary

In this chapter, I've stressed the importance of creating a positive environment for your presentation. Thoughtful attention to what may seem like minor details—the room, air quality and lighting, along with your appearance, introduction and use of audio-visuals—will give your presentation a distinctively superior quality.

Everything covered thus far has been designed to help you achieve a high level of self-confidence and excellence. Yet there is no greater enemy of excellence than fear. In the next chapter, I'll show you how you can transform fear in order to be the best that you can be.

Chapter 6 Mind Map

CHAPTER 7

Transforming Fear

Fear is the mind-killer, the little death.
Frank Herbert, in *Dune*

For as he thinks within himself, so he is.
Proverbs 23:7

Fear—a feeling of anxiety and agitation caused by the presence or nearness of danger, evil, pain, timidity, dread, terror, fright, apprehension.
Webster's Unabridged Dictionary

What is the "danger, evil and pain" associated with speaking to a group? What are people afraid of when they stand before their fellow humans?

The answer is simple. Humiliation. Embarrassment. Loss of self-esteem and dignity.

What are the origins of this fear?

Think back to your first few years of school. Perhaps you can recall when someone in your class enthusiastically stood up to recite, took his/her turn at 'show and tell', or answered a question and was greeted with paroxysms of mocking laughter. Both witnesses and victims of this typical scenario find that the fear of being laughed at—of being the subject of ridicule—becomes a powerful force that cripples self expression. Some of us come away from this kind of experience with a dread of standing in front of a group. Most of us just learn to give boring, mediocre presentations, bereft of creativity, in order to minimize the risk of being mocked.

The most experienced speakers will occasionally feel the symptoms of fear before and during a presentation. Even a veteran actress such as Helen Hayes—with over fifty years of experience on stage—still reports feeling butterflies in her stomach prior to a show.

In this chapter, I will introduce you to a practical approach that transforms fear into power and makes the butterflies 'fly in formation'.

The first point to understand is that there is nothing wrong with feeling fear. The key to success is knowing how to control your *reactions* to fear. When you understand how to control these reactions, you can transform the energy fear provides into a force that helps you to be your best.

In order to learn how to cope with fear, it is helpful to develop an understanding of the mechanism through which it operates.

The Startle Pattern

During the 1960s, Tufts University researcher Dr. Frank Pierce Jones conducted extensive research on the mechanism of fear. In one experiment, Jones tested a group of 1,000 people. He asked each to stand in his/her most comfortable posture and then proceeded to frighten them by making a sudden noise. He found, in every case, that the reactions were the same: to tighten the neck muscles, hold the breath, and contract the major joint surfaces of the body. He called this profile of tension the 'startle pattern'.

Jones observed that the startle pattern provided a model of reaction for responses to any stressful situation. In other words, most people react to stressful situations by stiffening their neck muscles, holding their breath and contracting their bodies. Jones's most critical observation was that due to the inordinate stresses of modern life, most

The Startle Pattern

adults become permanently trapped in a modified form of the startle pattern.[1]

As a result, most of us approach the act of presenting with fear already locked into our bodies. The startle pattern gradually becomes more pronounced as we worry about an imminent presentation. This reaction is insidious because it usually occurs below consciousness. Most of us don't become aware of our reaction until we are seized by gross manifestations of fear, such as sweating palms, pounding hearts and choking throats. At this point, fear controls us.

In order to take command of fear and reach our full potential, we need to find a method for freeing ourselves from both the chronic and acute effects of the startle pattern.

The Alexander Technique

The most effective method was developed by F. Mathias Alexander (1869-1955), a Shakespearean actor from Australia.[5] Alexander's successful stage career was threatened by a persistent, stress-related tendency to lose his voice in the middle of his performances. Working on his own, Alexander observed through the use of mirrors that as soon as he began to *think* about reciting, he tended to tighten his neck muscles, resulting in a pulling back of his head, interference with his breathing and a shortening of his stature. Alexander observed further that the manifestations of this pattern became more severe as he attempted to recite increasingly difficult passages. He reasoned that this pattern of interference (which Jones would later call the startle pattern) was responsible for causing the problems with his voice.[2]

Alexander eventually solved his problem by developing a technique for freeing himself from this habitual pattern of constriction, and soon became famous on the stage, renowned for his extraordinary voice and stage presence. People flocked to him for lessons, and as a result of their demand, he developed what came to be known as the Alexander Technique. This is usually taught through a series of individual lessons in which the teacher uses a very subtle form of manual guidance to lead the pupil to an enhanced experience of balance and poise.[3] As lessons progress, the student learns to recognize and prevent unnecessary patterns of tension, thereby discovering a more graceful, integrated manner of moving and speaking.

The Alexander Technique has become known as a trade secret among professional performers, and has been taught for years at many of the world's top academies of the performing arts, including the Julliard School of Music in New York and the Royal Academies of Drama and Music in England. The Technique is an integral part of the presentation courses I provide to educators and business people around the world.

The Alexander Technique cannot be learned fully from a book. There is one procedure drawn from Alexander's work, however, that you can begin practicing now. The procedure, which I call the Balanced Resting State, is used by Alexander teachers throughout the world. If practiced regularly, it helps free you from the effects of the startle pattern. The procedure is very simple; it takes about ten minutes. Use the instructions below, with reference to the illustration that follows.

The Balanced Resting State

1) Begin by placing a few books—between four to six inches in height—on a carpeted floor. Stand approximately your body's length away from the books (with your back toward them) and pause for a moment. Place your feet shoulder-width apart, your eyes facing straight ahead and your hands gently at your sides.

2) Think of allowing your body to lengthen and expand. You might, for example, imagine that there is a string attached to the top of your head, gently easing your head and spine up toward the ceiling. Breathing freely, become aware of the feeling of your feet on the floor and notice the distance from your feet to the top of your head. Keep your eyes focused and alive, and listen to the sounds around you.

3) Maintaining this awareness, move lightly and quickly so that you are resting on one knee. Then roll yourself back so that you are supporting yourself with your hands behind you, feet flat on the floor and knees bent. Continue breathing easily.

4) Let your head drop forward a tiny bit to ensure that you are not tightening your neck muscles; then gently roll your spine back along the floor so that your head is resting on the books, which should be positioned to support your head at the place where your neck ends and your head begins. If your head is not well-positioned on the books, reach back with one hand and support your head while using the other hand to place the books in the proper position. Your feet remain flat on the floor, with your knees pointing up to the ceiling, and your

The Balanced Resting State

hands rest easily at your sides or are gently folded on your chest. Allow your weight to be fully supported by the floor.

5) All you need to reap the benefit of this procedure is to rest in this position for approximately ten minutes. As you rest, gravity will be lengthening your spine and realigning your torso. Keep your eyes open to avoid dozing off. You may wish to bring your attention to your breathing and to the gentle pulsation of your whole body. Be aware of the ground supporting your back, allowing your shoulders to rest as your back widens. Let your whole body lengthen and expand.

6) After you have rested for ten minutes, get up slowly, being careful to avoid tightening or contracting your body as you return to a standing position. In order to facilitate this smooth transition, decide when you are going to move and then gently roll over onto your front, maintaining your new sense of integration. Ease your way into a crawling position, and then gently rise to standing.

7) Pause for a moment once you have reassumed the standing posture. Again, feel your feet on the floor, noticing the distance between your feet and the top of your head. You may be surprised to discover that the distance has expanded. As you move into the activities of your day or the presentation you're about to give, think about reinforcing this sense of expansion, ease and overall 'uplift'.

For best results, practice this a minimum of twice a day for ten minutes at a time. You can do it when you wake up in the morning and before retiring at night. The procedure is especially valuable when you feel overworked, or stressed, or when you are about to give a presentation. Regular practice will help you develop a sense of 'body confidence'—an upright, easy poise that will help you perform at your best.

Warm Up!

In addition to practicing the Balanced Resting State, there is something else you can do before every presentation—warming up—which will help you transform fear, and its accompanying stiffness and tension, into power and poise.

All too often, speakers ready themselves for presentations like condemned prisoners approaching the walk to the gallows. They sit still and stiffen up, imagining everything that could go wrong. Instead, find a place where you can move freely and practice as many of the following warm up exercises as you can.

Warm-Up Exercises

Wake up your eyes. Hold your index finger in front of your eyes and move it around, keeping your eyes focused on the tip of the finger. Move your finger randomly to the limits of your visual field. Do this as quickly as you can without moving your head. Practice for thirty seconds. It works even better if you can follow the shiny tip of a pen or the beam of a pocket flashlight. This exercise will wake up your eyes. When they are alive, bright and clearly focused, so are you.

Mobilize your face. Take a minute, in front of a mirror if possible, and make as many different faces as you can: funny, sad, angry, stupid, surprised, even frightened. Exaggerate each expression, making sure that your eyes are part of it. Scrunch your face tightly, and then make as big a face as possible with your eyes and mouth wide open. Hold each face for five seconds, relaxing for a moment in between. Do this five to ten times. Warming up your face in this manner allows you to feel more open and permits a greater range of expression.

Breathe. While sitting in a comfortable, upright position, become aware of the flow of your breath. Follow the movement of your breathing for thirty seconds without trying to change it. Then, allow yourself a deep, full inhalation followed by an extended, complete exhalation. Do this seven times, allowing each breath to be deeper than the one before. To enhance the effectiveness of this exercise further, make a deep, sighing 'ahhhh' sound as you exhale. This simple exercise is very powerful and relaxing. It will help you feel calm and energized at the same time.

Open your voice. Now that you are breathing freely, get your voice in gear. Experiment with yawning, sighing and humming. Sing vowel sounds in ascending and descending scales. Without straining, discover your highest and lowest notes. Sing or hum your favorite inspirational song. You can even try singing the first few minutes of your presentation. These simple voice exercises will help prevent you from choking up, as they enhance the quality and resonance of your voice.

Get your blood moving. Start by shaking your hands and feet vigorously. Then, using both hands, knead the top of your shoulders, the back of your neck and the top of your head. Follow this with a gentle massage of your forehead, temples and the orbits of each eye (being careful not to touch your eyeballs). Next massage your jaw, mush your cheeks around and pull on your ears.

Continue by using both hands to knead your legs vigorously up and down from your thighs to your ankles. Rub your abdomen in a clockwise motion and then reach your arms behind you to massage your lower back. You can also jog in place, juggle, dance or practice your favorite stretching exercise; whatever works best to get your blood flowing.

As you practice these warm up exercises, you will find your fear and stiffness transformed into enthusiasm and freedom. Remember to reinforce your positive visualization of your presentation. Imagine yourself presenting in a relaxed and competent manner. Let your energy flow. What you used to call 'fear' can now be renamed excitement and anticipation.

Comforting Thoughts

In addition to the practical exercises described above, a number of comforting thoughts can be useful allies in transforming fear.

Inexperienced speakers often imagine that audiences will take malicious delight in their slightest error. And, as in some vaudevillian nightmare, their first mistake will cause them to be 'hooked' off the stage to a chorus of jeers. This will not happen. Audiences are almost always extremely tolerant and sympathetic.

Remember that *your audience wants you to succeed.* They are attending your presentation with the hope of benefiting from it, so your success is in their best interest. Most audience members feel a natural empathy with the speaker and will tend to be supportive if any difficulties occur.

Also, remember that *your audience is made up of individuals not unlike yourself.* There is a tendency among presenters to look upon an audience as a common mass—which, in its impersonality, makes them more fearful. This tendency is exacerbated as group size increases. Whatever the size of your group, remember that it is made up of individual human beings. Never allow yourself to be intimidated by them. If you find yourself losing this perspective, look at their faces and imagine what they looked like in their first grade class photos. This is an amusing and surefire way of eliminating intimidation.

In addition, consider that as a presenter, *you are in a situation of power and control* with respect to an audience. Enjoy it! You have been invited to take command of the moment, and if you respond to the opportunity, you will find yourself in a dynamic, powerful position.

When you stand before a group, your sense of time is altered by the effect of adrenaline as it races through your bloodstream. Time speeds up, and it becomes all too easy to interpret your slightest nervous gesture or misspoken word in a grossly exaggerated manner. Your audience, however, is operating on 'normal time' and what seems a glaring mistake to you will often pass unnoticed by them.

Remember that even if you are very nervous, *you will almost always look better than you feel.* Participants in my presentation skills programs almost invariably underestimate their impact in trial presentations. When they watch a videotape of their efforts, they are often pleasantly surprised to find they looked better than they had imagined.

The simplest way to free yourself from fear is to *focus primarily on your audience and their needs.* Excess nervousness and self-consciousness feed off each other in a vicious cycle. When nervous, we tend to focus too much on ourselves and all our weaknesses. This negative focus creates more nervousness. . . Alternatively, if you keep your attention focused on the needs of your audience and your commitment to fulfilling your objectives, you won't have time or cause to worry.

**A Lighthearted Look
at Your Audience**

Finally, *most audiences have come to expect a very low standard of presentation*. People are exposed regularly to lifeless, unimaginative presentations that seem to drone on interminably. Because you care enough about excellence to have read this far, you will undoubtedly rise well above the average audience's expectation!

Summary

In order to transform fear, you must first recognize that there is nothing wrong with feeling fear—it is a universal phenomenon. Your reaction to fear is what's important. Secondly, become familiar with the manifestations of the startle pattern and begin to free yourself from it by studying the Alexander Technique and practicing the Balanced Resting State. Thirdly, remember to warm up before every presentation. Use the warm-up exercises described in this chapter or make up your own. And finally, remember these comforting thoughts: your audience wants you to succeed; they are human beings like you; you are in a position of power and control; you are probably better than you think; you are less nervous when you focus primarily on your audience; and *you* are likely to exceed their expectations!

As we have seen through the consideration of the startle pattern, fear manifests itself through our bodies. And through the application of the Alexander Technique, we can learn to use our bodies in ways that can help us in transforming that fear. In the next chapter, we'll explore the powerful role that your body plays in communication and how to make the most of it.

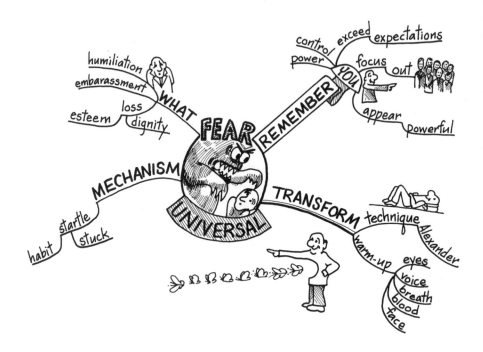

Chapter 7 Mind Map

Chapter 8

Let Your Body Talk

He who knows that power is inborn. . .and so perceiving, throws himself unhesitatingly on his thought, instantly rights himself, stands in the erect position, commands his limbs, works miracles.
Ralph Waldo Emerson,
Self-Reliance

Let your own discretion be your tutor: suit the action to the word, the word to the action.
Shakespeare, *Hamlet*

Your 'body language' —posture, movement, gestures, eye contact and voice—has a tremendous impact on your audience. When you address a group of people, they are constantly responding, consciously and unconsciously, to what your body is 'saying' to them. Research shows that fifty-five percent of your presentation's impact is determined by your posture, gestures and eye contact; thirty-eight percent by your voice tone and inflection; and only seven percent by the content of your presentation.[1]

Yet, habit or fear lead many presenters to hide their bodies behind podiums or lecterns, becoming no more than 'talking heads' to their audiences. If you wish to communicate with maximum impact, you must emerge from behind the podium and discover how to make the most of your body language.

Distracting body language such as constricted posture, unconscious swaying movements, pencil fondling, averted eyes and frequent 'ums'

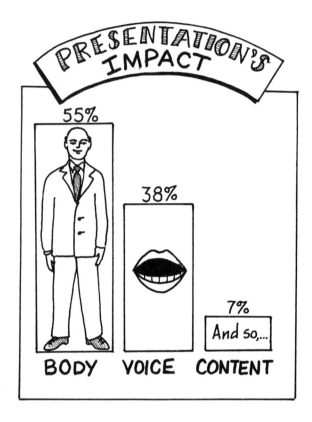

BODY   VOICE   CONTENT

and 'uhs' will interfere with the integrity of your communication. On the other hand, a relaxed, upright posture, a purposeful economy of movement, fluid gestures, lively eyes and an expressive voice will capture an audience's attention and greatly enhance the power of your message.

If your body language is not synchronized with your message, you lose credibility. In the words of the old Chinese proverb, "Watch out for the man whose stomach doesn't move when he laughs!"

In this chapter, I will show you how to eliminate distracting, unnecessary elements of your body language while making the most of what remains.

Developing Articulate Body Language

In order to develop articulate body language, begin by understanding that all its main elements—posture, movement, gestures, eye contact and voice—are intimately related and interdependent. For example, if your posture is rigid, it leads to stiffness in your movement, tightness in your voice and restriction of your gestures. More than any particular element, *it is the overall coordination of the various components of your body language—with the message you are attempting to communicate—that is of primary importance.* In order to build this 'body-message synchrony', however, we must begin by treating each of the elements of body language separately.

The Elements of Body Language

Posture. Your posture is the most fundamental statement you make with your body. An aligned, upright posture communicates a message of confidence and integrity. It says that you are 'together' and 'on the level'. Yet most people's posture is either collapsed, marked by a concave chest and slumping shoulders, or rigid, with a stiff neck and raised shoulders. What kind of message do these postures communicate?

An integrated body posture—one that will communicate positively to an audience—is balanced, upright and effortless.

I know of no better way to develop such a posture than to study the Alexander Technique and to practice the Balanced Resting State explained in the previous chapter. One can also learn from other disciplines, such as the martial arts and various athletic activities in which participants cultivate a 'basic posture' as a point of departure for all movement.

In the same way, you will want to develop a basic posture for presenting—a stance that will give you a solid grounding for all your body language.

The basic posture. Begin by practicing the Balanced Resting State. Then, standing in front of a mirror, place your feet approximately shoulder-length apart. Rest your hands at your sides. Stand upright, with your shoulders resting easily on your torso. Imagine your back 'smiling' as you sense the floor supporting you. Use the mirror to give you feedback on your alignment and your success in avoiding unnecessary, fidgeting movements. Practice standing quietly—without stiffening—for thirty seconds at a time. As you become comfortable with this basic stance, you can begin practicing it while engaged in casual conversation.

The Basic Posture

This simple posture is incredibly powerful, as many actors who have worked years to master it will tell you. It projects confidence and power. Audiences become more receptive and responsive when you stand before them so calmly and with such pure dignity.

Movement. With an integrated, basic posture as your point of departure, you are better able to realize your potential for communicating through movement.

Audiences are either distracted or attracted by all the movements that you make. Unnecessary, unconscious movements, such as swaying, rocking or pacing will distract and annoy the audience. Awareness is the key to freeing yourself from these unnecessary movements and is best cultivated by watching yourself on video (or in a large mirror if video is unavailable). As your awareness increases, you will find it easier to move in a natural, expressive manner.

Moving in relaxed coordination with what you are saying not only engages your audience, but also prevents you from stiffening, as often happens when one sits or stands in one place for too long. Examples of natural, expressive movements might include walking toward your audience when emphasizing a point, or walking away, leaving them to contemplate a question you have just posed.

Make all your movements purposeful. If you are not sure of where or how to move, then return to your basic posture.

Gesture. Just as a conductor uses a baton to synchronize the orchestra, you can employ gestures to help conduct your message to the brains of your audience. When used appropriately, gestures provide another 'wavelength' upon which an audience can receive your communication.

Gestures can be tremendously powerful. To take full advantage of this power, it is essential that you *avoid unnecessary gestures* that rob your message of its impact. Examples include habits such as pencil fondling, table tapping, handwringing, haircurling and hand-in-pocket change rattling.

Your gestures must be natural, expressive and clear. Attempts to teach a particular set of gestures, however, are doomed to failure because the essence of effective gestural communication is spontaneity and authenticity. Gestures must emerge naturally from within you, rather than being imposed from the outside. When people are trained to use a particular pattern of gestures, they usually seem robotic, stilted and insincere.

In my presentation workshops, I help each student discover his/her own gestural vocabulary. One of my favorite examples concerns a manager of a large Swedish shipping company. He held his hands about four inches apart when describing his company's largest tanker. A shy man, his four inch gesture probably felt big—a useful gestural description of a giant tanker. If he had been told that the gesture was ludicrously small and urged to hold his hands wider apart, he would have felt uncomfortable and given an even more stilted impression. I asked him to look at the video of his presentation to see if he was accurately depicting a big tanker. His laughter immediately suggested that he recognized the insufficiency of his gesture. He tried again, making a gesture twice the size. Again, he looked at the video and saw that he still wasn't doing justice to the pride of his company's fleet. After a few more takes, he extended his hands fully, and his voice boomed: "Ve haf really big tanker!" while his colleagues applauded wildly.

Develop your gestural vocabulary by playing with the following exercises I use with my students. Do these in front of a mirror or—better yet—a video camera.

Experiment with different gestures to help you communicate each of the following phrases. Create your own context for each one. Say each phrase out loud as you make the gesture. And have fun!

► Today, I will be covering three major points. . .

► We'll be developing this project from the ground up.

► If you agree, please raise your hand.

► Let's all stand up and have a stretch.

► We sell the biggest system in the industry for the smallest price.

► She placed it sixteen inches down from the upper left hand corner of the rear wall, next to the one he placed there yesterday.

And now for the advanced portion of the exercise. Experiment with your gestures while reciting the following (remember to say each quote aloud):

► This is the true joy in life. The being used for a purpose, recognized by yourself as a mighty one; the being thoroughly worn out before you are thrown on the scrap heap; the being a force of nature instead of a feverish, selfish little clod of ailments and grievances, complaining that the world will not devote itself to making you happy. — George Bernard Shaw.

► No one who, like me, conjures up the most evil of those half tamed demons who inhabit the human breast and seeks to wrestle with them, can expect to come through the struggle unscathed. — Sigmund Freud.

► Speak the speech, I pray you, as I pronounced it to you, trippingly on the tongue...nor do not saw the air too much with your hand, thus, but use all gently; for in the very torrent, tempest, and, as I may say, the whirlwind of passion, you must acquire and beget a temperance that may give it smoothness...be not too tame neither, but let your own discretion be your tutor, suit your action to the word, and your word to the action. — William Shakespeare.

In addition to practicing the above exercise—which you can develop and expand on your own—take every opportunity to study gesture in everyday communication. Observe others, noticing the ratio between effective and unnecessary gestures. Watch television without the sound. Play charades. One of the best exercises is to observe or, better yet, study American sign language—the language used by deaf people.[2] And finally, practice delivering your whole presentation without using any words at all!

Eye contact. Imagine that you are waiting to make a turn at a stop light. The driver of a car in the next lane turns to make eye contact with you, indicating the desire to move in front of you. Your eyes meet. Do you let him in? Chances are, unless you're in a rotten mood, that you do.

Eye contact is a humanizing element in an often impersonal world. It is a crucial aspect of communication and, thus, an important part of every successful presentation.

Eye contact should be a simple, natural expression of your interest in the audience. It allows you to monitor their level of interest and understanding of your message. Making eye contact with your audience also draws their attention—helping them feel more personally involved.

As I mentioned in the previous chapter, however, speakers often suffer under the delusion that their audience is an impersonal mass and that eye contact with individuals is therefore impossible. The inability to make eye contact may also be caused by fear, lack of confidence or simply thinking too much about oneself instead of the audience.

You can develop your innate ability to make contact and communicate with your eyes by experimenting with the following:

► Look in the mirror and express these feelings and emotions using only your eyes:

surprise, anger, skepticism, intrigue, intensity, love, confusion, confidence, irony, boredom, fear, playfulness, sincerity and wonder.

If possible, practice this exercise with a friend, guessing which of the feelings is being communicated. Have fun making up additional material.

► Practice looking people in the eye in ordinary conversation. Experiment with holding the eye contact a little bit longer than usual. But remember, it's the quality of the contact that counts more than the duration.

► When you enter a room, particularly prior to a presentation, look around and make eye contact with as many people as you can.

► While delivering your presentation, make regular eye contact with the friendliest looking person on each side and in the middle of the room. This will help you become more comfortable with eye contact, and you'll find it easier to make contact with other members of the audience. Practicing this exercise will also help you avoid being lured, by the friendly eyes of one person, into the common trap of directing your whole presentation to one part of the room.

► As your confidence builds, experiment with making regular eye contact with the unfriendliest looking person on either side and in the middle of the room. See if you can draw them out with your eyes as you speak.

Perhaps more than any other element, eye contact reflects your interest in your audience and determines your level of rapport with them.

Voice. Research shows that a major portion of the impact of your presentation stems from the way you use your voice.[3] It is your primary tool of communication and has the potential to be tremendously expressive. You can, with your voice alone, communicate many shades of meaning. Consider, for example, how much information can be gleaned from the tone of the first word spoken in a telephone conversation.

Your voice, like your posture, gestures, movement and eye contact, should be natural, expressive and clear. You can refine your voice by recognizing and eliminating unnecessary elements in your vocal usage. In order to do this, you must first learn how to pause.

Learn to pause. Great musicians have often stated that it is not so much the way in which a note is played as the pauses between the notes that create their art. So it is with the speaking voice.

Pausing is a natural part of speaking. Yet, anxiety often causes speakers to fill their pauses with uhmms, uhhhs, you knows and other unnecessary, distracting noises. A powerful, expressive speaking rhythm is characterized by frequent, complete pauses. *Learning to pause appropriately is the single most important element in making the most of your voice.*

Pausing gives you the opportunity to think about what to say next and to hear what you just said. A pause gives you time to collect yourself and breathe fully. It also gives your audience time to assimilate your message and feel more relaxed. Furthermore, an appropriate pause actually draws an audience's attention and interest.

In order to develop your ability to pause appropriately, you must first of all realize that *your audience welcomes the pause.* Secondly, don't be afraid to make your pause complete. Remember that the flow of adrenaline will tend to speed up your sense of time so that a pause, which may seem like an eternity to you, is barely noticeable to the audience. Finally, experiment by speaking into a tape recorder, varying and extending your pauses, leaving out the uhmms and uhhhs, and remembering to breathe. Then listen to your voice on the tape in order to develop your sense of when and how to pause.

Pausing and Pacing. Many speakers talk too fast, often speeding up as their speech progresses. This can cause poor articulation, slurring or swallowing of words and a loss of contact with the audience. Speedtalking usually occurs because of nervousness or over-excitement. Never allow yourself to be hurried as you speak, even if you are short on time. If you find that your time is running out, trim your less crucial content rather than talking faster. Whatever the cause, the best remedy for talking too fast is to pause regularly. Pausing allows you to breathe and collect yourself, and makes it much easier to take your time.

The great opera singer Nellie Melba once said that the voice can be used three ways. It can be held in, forced out, or it may be given to an audience easily and graciously. In addition to pausing, there are several other important considerations for learning to use your voice easily and graciously.

Tone and inflection. Your voice is a naturally expressive instrument. The movement of tone and inflection gives your voice its expressive life. Suppressing this natural movement results in monotony, which is deadening—one of the surest ways to put your audience to sleep. It is a way of anesthetizing oneself against fear, rather than facing it and using the heightened energy as an expressive force.

Another common way of interfering with natural expressiveness is to distort it by being phony. Nervousness often causes speakers to 'posture' their voices in a constrained and artificial manner, leading them to try too hard to give a particular impression. The irony is that *trying* to sound authoritative, for example, communicates a lack of trust in one's own authority. Other common examples include trying to sound nice, sincere or profound.

In many cases, distortion of the voice is caused or perpetuated by excessive, chronic tension of the jaw. The jaw tends to be a centerpoint of stress for most people. Learning to free the jaw, therefore, is a crucial element in liberating one's voice. The following exercises will help you increase your awareness of jaw tension and begin releasing it, thus enhancing your natural sense of tone and inflection.

▶ Begin by reading the following quote while exaggerating the tension in your jaw. Listen carefully to the quality of your voice while reading. Use a tape recorder if possible.

Thirty spokes are made one by holes in a hub,
By vacancies joining them for a wheel's use;
The use of clay in molding pitchers
Comes from the hollow of its absence;
Doors, windows in a house,
Are used for their emptiness;
Thus we are helped by what is not,
to use what is.
                    Lao Tsu, *The Tao Te Ching*

▶ Next, place your index finger in between your upper and lower molars on one side of your mouth for thirty seconds. Then, allow your jaw to drop freely without the help of your finger for another thirty seconds. This will help you discover the natural drop of your jaw. When you first do this exercise, you will probably feel like an idiot. Practice regularly, until it feels comfortable and natural to release your jaw in this manner.

► Grasp your chin firmly, and gently waggle your jaw up and down for one minute. Be certain to move only your jaw, keeping your head still.

► Now, read the Lao Tsu quote again and notice the difference in your voice quality.

The regular practice of these jaw release exercises will help your natural sense of tone and inflection to emerge. You can further explore your vocal expressiveness by playing with the following exercises.

Say "hello," in a way that communicates each of the following feelings:

surprise, anger, skepticism, intrigue, intensity, love, confusion, confidence, irony, boredom, fear, playfulness, sincerity and wonder.

Do the exercise again, this time using the phrase:

"The report is due on Tuesday."

For the advanced part of the exercise, express *all* of the feelings listed in one recitation of the following:

Have more than thou showest,
Speak less that thou knowest,
Lend less than thou owest,
Ride more than thou goest,*
Learn more than thou trowest,**
***Set less than thou throwest,
And thou shalt have more
Than two tens to a score.

William Shakespeare,
King Lear

(*goest—walk; **trowest—to know; ***set—stake)

Practice these exercises with a friend, guessing which of the feelings is being communicated. Enjoy making up additional material.

Develop volume control. In order to make full use of your expressive abilities, be certain that the audience can hear what you're saying. If you're not sure you can be heard (or if you think you are speaking too loudly), ask your audience for feedback and modulate your volume accordingly.

Raising and lowering your voice appropriately is essential to effective speaking. It allows you greater scope for emphasizing your message and enhances your expressiveness. Use the following exercise to practice modulating your voice appropriately. Notice the effects of volume on your vocal expressiveness as you practice.

Read the following poem four times: in a whisper; in an ordinary conversational tone; as though you were speaking to a group of ten people; and then to a group of fifty people (speak easily and graciously—don't strain your voice).

> *Awaken each clause with tender pause.*
> *Recite each section with tone and inflection;*
> *And speak each word so it can be heard!*
> Anonymous.

In addition to the exercises I've introduced in this section, you can also develop greater flexibility and expressiveness in your voice by singing, learning other languages and by mimicking various accents.

Body-Message Synchrony

Having considered the elements of body language individually, now put them all together. Observe the effects of various gestures on your voice tone. Notice how your posture affects your movement and eye contact. Try any of the exercises above, noting the coordination between all the elements of your body language.

Of all the elements discussed in this chapter, posture is most fundamental. A balanced, upright posture opens your voice, frees movement and gesture and enhances alertness, thereby encouraging better eye contact. Remember, however, that by working on any of the elements of body language, you are working on them all.

Most importantly, be aware of the synchrony between the elements of body language and your message. When words say one thing, and body language another, the result is an impression of confusion, insincerity or deceit. For example, in his debate with President Reagan, Walter Mondale tried to capture his adversary's constituency by emphasizing a strong national defense. Mondale was clearly coached to use the word 'strength' frequently and to pound his fist on the podium everytime he said it. Unfortunately for the Democrats, Mondale's fist-pounding was weak and unconvincing, accompanied by his voice cracking and a slight aversion of his gaze. This inconsistency of body language and message was a key factor in his defeat by the Great Communicator. Politics can provide many amusing opportunities for observing variations in the relationship between body language and message.

The study of salespeople provides another fascinating theatre for observing the importance of body-message synchrony. Salespeople are all too often characterized as crooked or beady-eyed. Each of these terms refers to a fundamental lack of integrity expressed through their bodies. The finest salespeople know that the ultimate key to success is believing in themselves and their products, a belief that is communicated through the integrity of their body language.

The only way to ensure body-message synchrony is to be honest with yourself and your audience. There is no substitute for authenticity.

Summary

The information and exercises in this chapter are designed to help you unleash your tremendous capacity for vibrant, powerful communication. A balanced, upright posture, dynamic movement, animated gestures, lively eyes and expressive voice are all part of your birthright. As emphasized throughout this chapter, the key to gaining access to your natural expressiveness is to *leave out the unnecessary* elements that interfere with it. This will come with practice, experience and a commitment to authenticity.

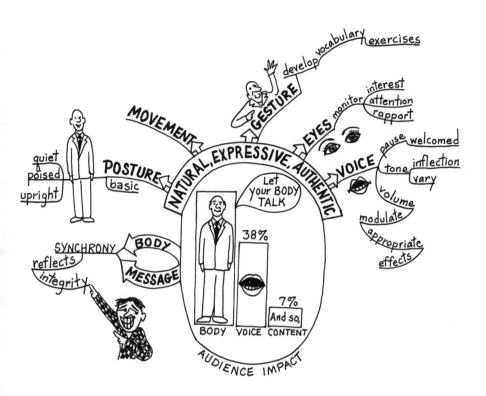

Chapter 8 Mind Map

Michelangelo created some of his greatest sculptures by seeing the perfect form inside the stone. All the information and exercises in this book are designed to help you emerge fully and present yourself in the simplest, least cosmetic way possible. You now have all the tools you need to reach a peak of confidence and self-assurance.

Take the elements and put them all together.

Your audiences are waiting to see and hear you.

Put your best foot forward. PRESENT YOURSELF!

In the next chapter, I'll give you some hints on how to continue your development as a presenter.

Mind Map Summary of Present Yourself!

CHAPTER 9

Better and Better

In order to succeed, double your failure rate.
Thomas Watson, president
and founder, IBM

Just before he died, the great artist Auguste Renoir completed his final painting. His last words were, "I think I'm beginning to understand something about [art]." Renoir possessed the essential quality that is characteristic of all true high performers—a life-long commitment to learning.

The more knowledge and experience you have in a given area, the easier it becomes to learn more. At the same time, as your knowledge and experience increase, so does your awareness of the vast amount that remains to be learned. This is why the wise are often humble.

Whatever your current level as a presenter, there is more for you to learn and unlimited potential for improvement. To tap your full potential, you must commit yourself to getting better and better, recognizing that you have an opportunity to improve every time you present.

In this chapter are some simple strategies which will help you continue your development as a high performance presenter.

The Road to Excellence

Feed your visualization of excellence. Think of yourself as a superior presenter, regularly building and refining your visualization of excellence. Be on the lookout for anything that can help you improve your presentations: observe other excellent presenters whenever possible; look for facts, stories, literary references, parables, audio-visuals— anything you can use to update and improve your material and delivery.

Take every opportunity to present. Practice every chance you get; there is no substitute for experience. Tell stories and jokes to friends. Give informal talks to anyone who will listen. Join your local chapter of Toastmasters or the National Speakers Association.[1]

Seek feedback. Consider how a baby learns. It absorbs all the data it can with enthusiasm and wonder—instantly translating 'mistakes' into learning experiences and thus learning at remarkable speed without losing self-confidence. Cultivate this same high-performance learning attitude while seeking feedback on your presentations.

Do your best to discover what kind of impact you have on an audience. If appropriate, hand out evaluation forms, ask questions of audience members or invite trusted friends or colleagues to attend your presentations for the purpose of giving you detailed feedback. An accurate critique is the greatest gift you can receive.

One of the finest ways to ensure high quality feedback is to set up a buddy system with a trusted friend or colleague who shares your commitment to high performance. I personally have used this system over a period of more than twelve years with great success. Arrange to attend as many of each other's presentations as you possibly can and to make comprehensive notes on one another's performances (you can use the presentations journal described later in this chapter as a guide for your notes).

Plan a time to meet and exchange feedback, using the following procedure. Ask your partner to begin by focusing only on those aspects of your presentation that, in his opinion, could be improved. The feedback should be kept ruthlessly honest, objective and specific. When receiving your critique, take notes and don't explain or defend yourself. Ask questions only to gain further clarity. This form of listening allows you to get unusually pure feedback. Once the focus on your weaknesses has been completed (take a maximum of fifteen minutes), do the same exercise, this time focusing on your strengths. Again, it is important to listen without responding to gain a full appreciation and understanding of what you did well.

The feedback exercise is tremendously powerful, and if you practice it faithfully, with a perceptive and sensitive partner, it will lead you to insights about your presentations that would otherwise be impossible. As you develop skill in critiquing your partner's presentation, your model of excellence will grow exponentially.

Keep a presentations journal. Create a journal to help you plan and evaluate your presentations. Use this journal to record information about the audience, your objectives, the environment and your content before you present. After each presentation, objectively evaluate your strengths and weaknesses and record them. You can use the following questions and format as a guide for building your own comprehensive high-performance presentations journal. Reviewing your journal regularly will hone your 'high performance mind set' while speeding your progress.

Presentations Journal

A. PREPARATION

Use this section in preparing for your presentation, then review it afterwards and add comments. Include:

► A Mind Map of the presentation.

► Key facts about the audience (number of people, expectations, gender, etc.).

► Objectives for this presentation:
How will success be measured?

► Possible questions or objections from the audience.

► Starting time:
Finishing time:

► Introduction arranged?

► Logistics coordinated by?

► Environmental checklist completed?

CHECKLIST   ## COMMENTS

_____ Lighting   _____

_____ Air quality
and temperature   _____

_____ Furniture   _____

_____ Microphone   _____

_____ AV Equipment   _____

_____ Music   _____

_____ No Smoking signs   _____

_____ Plants   _____

_____ Flowers   _____

_____ Acoustics   _____

_____ Miscellaneous   _____

▶ Warm-up exercises (space and time arranged?)

B. FEEDBACK

Record your comments and, where appropriate, rate yourself in each area on a 1 (low) to 10 (high) scale.

▶ Objectives accomplished   1 2 3 4 5 6 7 8 9 10
Comments:

▶ Use of audio-visuals   1 2 3 4 5 6 7 8 9 10
Comments:

► Posture   1 2 3 4 5 6 7 8 9 10
Comments:

► Gesture   1 2 3 4 5 6 7 8 9 10
Comments:

► Movement   1 2 3 4 5 6 7 8 9 10
Comments:

► Voice   1 2 3 4 5 6 7 8 9 10
Comments:

► Overall body language   1 2 3 4 5 6 7 8 9 10
Comments:

► Major weaknesses of my presentation:

► Major strengths:

► What would I do differently next time?

► My own comfort and enjoyment level:

► General comments:

Keep your journal in a special file along with your Mind Maps and any evaluation forms you receive. Even if you don't record this information, you can still benefit by asking yourself the journal questions after each presentation.

There is one other essential point that has been implicit throughout this book: Above all, the key to giving great presentations is having fun. So, practice, enjoy and have fun!

CHAPTER 10

Twenty Questions and Answers

When I lead seminars on presentation skills, the participants always ask me excellent questions. Since you may have similar questions after reading *Present Yourself!*, I'd like to try to anticipate and answer some of them here.

1) *The organization where I work is very conservative—and some of your suggestions on how I can make my presentations more creative may be too controversial for my superiors and co-workers. Under these circumstances, how can I make my presentations better?*

Balance your creativity with logic and sensitivity to your organization's culture. Gauge your organization's comfort zone objectively—not from a position of fear, which will cause you to underestimate their receptivity to new ideas. Then, try to work within and gently stretch this 'comfort zone'. You don't have to be P.T. Barnum to give superior presentations; just remember what makes people—in any context—pay attention and remember, and present yourself accordingly.

2) *How much time should I give myself to properly rehearse a presentation?*

There is no set minimum or maximum amount of time—rehearse until you are confident. Set your objectives, then generate, organize and become comfortable with your material as soon as you can. This will give you more time to experiment with creative ways to deliver your message.

3) *What if I have to give a presentation on very short notice?*

In order to succeed under pressure, you must maintain your poise and act confidently. You must not allow yourself to be undermined by fear. It is essential that you begin immediately to visualize a successful out-come. Use Mind Mapping to generate ideas and organize your content and objectives, then practice the Mind Map Memory Method.

4) *If I have to give many presentations in a short space of time, how do I prevent burn-out?*

Be sensitive to your own energy level. The excitement and adrenaline rush of successful presentations can obscure your awareness of your own exhaustion. It takes a lot of energy to give effective presentations. If you are on a busy speaking schedule, you must take good care of your-self to prevent 'burn-out'. As with other performance professionals (ath-letes, actors, dancers, etc.) you must sleep well, exercise regularly and eat a healthy, balanced diet. I cannot overemphasize the importance of these three elements.

It is also essential that you take regular breaks even in the midst of a demanding schedule. When you are speaking to groups day after day, you must give yourself regular periods of absolute quiet. Make a point of finding a time when you won't have to talk to anyone. This will not only help to save your voice, it may also save your sanity. And, when you give your audience a break during sessions, don't always stay around to answer questions—leave the room and take a rejuvenating walk.

5) *How do I maintain my enthusiasm when I have to give the same presen-tation repeatedly?*

Every presentation is a learning opportunity for you. Take advantage of that fact, and you will never be bored. Also, remember that it's the first time for your audience. Think of them...

6) *What should I remember in making presentations to people more senior than me?*

Remember that you have been invited to address them for a reason. Take charge and present yourself with confidence. Generally, the more senior people are, the better they respond to those who conduct themselves in an authoritative manner. Never apologize for being there. Make sure that you dress immaculately and, if necessary, visualize how everyone in your audience looked in their first grade class photos!

7) *If for some reason I'm confronted with an unfavorable environment (too hot, stuffy, poor lighting, etc.) for my presentation, what can I do to make the best of the situation?*

If the environment is unfavorable, and there is nothing you can do to change it, acknowledge the circumstances in a light-hearted fashion and give your group more frequent breaks.

8) *Do you have any advice about how to make presentations to children?*

Treat them in the same manner you would an adult audience—with respect. Children will probably need more frequent breaks in order to release their abundant physical energy. Get them involved and active whenever possible. Keep your language simple and remember that, like an audience of adults, their brains will respond to color, imagery and metaphor—so apply these elements liberally.

9) *What should I do if I draw a blank in the middle of my presentation?*

If you've prepared thoroughly for your presentation, you won't experience this very often. However, even the most well-prepared presenters occasionally experience a sudden loss of place or a mental block. Your strength, therefore, will lie in how you handle the situation. When you recognize that you've lost your place, *pause for a moment*, breathe deeply and collect yourself. If your train of thought does not immediately return, you can simply ask your audience, "Where was I?" At which point, someone in the group will undoubtedly respond. This kind of honesty and directness will enhance your rapport with the audience.

10) *What are the most common mistakes presenters make?*

Not preparing thoroughly. Forgetting about the audience. Not giving enough breaks. Going on too long. Hiding behind audio-visuals. Apologizing. Speaking in a monotone. And, most importantly, underestimating themselves.

11) *Do you have any special advice for presenting on television?*

Remember that when you look into a television camera and speak to millions of people, you are speaking to millions of *individuals*. Talk as though you were speaking directly to any one of them. Exaggerate your gestures and don't worry about coming on too strong.

12) *How can I handle difficult people?*

Most difficult people are difficult because they have a problem. Often it has nothing to do with you and your presentation. Some people are insecure and just like to show off their knowledge; others may have gotten up on the wrong side of the bed that day. A few may be actually reacting to some aspect of your presentation. These problems can manifest themselves in anything from noisy paper shuffling to unnecessary or hostile questions. The best way to address these situations is, first of all, not to take them personally. Try to determine what the real issue is and deal with it if possible.

When handling aggressive questions, listen carefully and find something in what the questioner is saying that you can agree with. Avoid getting defensive. The better you are at empathizing, the easier it will be to defuse the situation. Don't let yourself get caught in a battle, even if you are sure you can overwhelm your 'opponent' with superior knowledge. You may win the battle but lose your audience. Maintain your rapport with the audience, and you will find that they will be effectively self-policing, not tolerating significant disruption by a disgruntled member.

Finally, bear in mind that if you are well-prepared and present yourself with confidence and authority, these kinds of problems will rarely arise.

13) *Can you give me some guidance on answering questions?*

Always listen carefully for the essence of what is being asked and treat every question with respect. Make sure that the question is heard by everyone, repeating it if necessary. It's a good idea to pause and think about the question before answering. Answer concisely. If you do not know the answer, you can refer the question to the group. This is often a good idea even when you do know as it encourages group involvement. Otherwise, say "I don't know" with authority, and offer to seek the answer and provide it at some future time.

14) *Is it possible to be a high-performance presenter if I am physically disabled?*

Certainly. Your honesty, integrity and willingness to reach out to your audience will determine your success.

15) *Can you give some guidance on making sales presentations?*

Be very clear about your own objectives. Know your audience. (Do they have the power to make the decision you want them to make?) Know what they want and need, and give it to them. Be sensitive to the moment when your audience is 'sold' and don't go on beyond that point. Instead, ask for the sale.

16) *Is it possible to apply a high-performance approach in schools?*

Absolutely. The best teachers have always intuitively practiced this approach by combining logic and discipline with imagination and fun. One of my favorite examples is the story of the winner of a statewide Teacher of the Year Award, whom I once saw on the evening news. Her class was studying the Salem Witch Trials, and the interview began with the teacher screaming into the room on a skateboard, dressed in a pointed black hat, cackling wildly. The children in her class were all dressed in period costumes and were absorbed in acting out scenes from the trial. The interviewer asked the children a number of challenging questions about the Trials, which they all answered effortlessly and correctly. She asked the children if they enjoyed this class, and the answer was a resounding, "It's the best class we've ever had!" As the interview progressed, the children were asked if they thought their teacher was strict, and they replied that she was the strictest, fairest and most demanding in the school.

The children were learning a tremendous amount, loved their teacher and were having fun. The high-performance approach balances logic and imagination, discipline and fun. This is what education should be!

17) *How should I use humor?*

Humor can be a marvelous tool for diffusing stressful situations, relaxing yourself and your audience, and for helping people to remember. Spontaneous humor works best, so avoid 'canned' jokes, and instead cultivate an appropriate light-heartedness.

18) *How can I learn more about the Alexander Technique?*

The Alexander Technique is best learned through individual lessons with a qualified teacher. Lessons usually last from thirty to forty-five minutes. Most teachers recommend a basic course of at least thirty lessons.

To find a qualified Alexander teacher in your area, write to:

The North American Society of Teachers of the Alexander Technique, P.O. Box 148026, Chicago, Illinois 60614-8026.

or to:

The Society of Teachers of the Alexander Technique, 10 London House, 266 Fulham Road, London SW10, ENGLAND.

19) *What are some other applications of Mind Mapping?*

Mind Mapping has hundreds of practical applications. Some of my favorites include planning vacations, parties, schedules and meetings; recording lectures, dreams, phone calls and study material; generating ideas for poetry and other creative endeavors; solving problems; and resolving conflicts. Last, but not least, Mind Maps are tremendously valuable tools for generating and organizing material for writing—articles, reports, books, etc. This book was written entirely from Mind Maps!

Beyond its value in improving your productivity, Mind Mapping helps you develop a balance between your logical and imaginative thinking capacities, thereby enhancing your mental flexibility and overall creativity.

20) *Will developing a high performance approach to presenting affect other aspects of my life?*

My experience shows that learning to present yourself is a tremendously powerful vehicle for self-development. In order to fundamentally improve your ability to express yourself to a group, you must grow as a human being. Be prepared to face your fears, insecurities and limiting habit patterns. Learn to place your ego on the shelf as you actively seek feedback on your performance.

As you meet these challenges, you will gain valuable insights into the nature of yourself and others. These insights will help you develop your skills in leadership and personal relationships, and will ultimately enhance your sense of self-confidence, poise and personal power.

Chapter Notes

Introduction

1. Tony Buzan-personal communication. See also *The Brain Users Guide*, (E.P. Dutton, New York, 1986). Buzan makes this assertion based on his assessment of the increase in the number of scientific papers published on the brain.

2. Wallace and Wallechinsky, *The Book of Lists*, (William Morrow and Company, New York, 1977), pg. 469. Fear of public speaking is rated the number one fear of 41% of the population in this survey, surpassing nuclear war, death, and financial ruin.

Chapter 1: Meet Your Brain

1. Tony Buzan, *Use Both Sides of Your Brain*, (E.P. Dutton, New York, 1985). See Chapter entitled "Your Mind Is Better Than You Think."

2. Peter Russell, *The Brain Book*, (Routledge and Kegan Paul, London, 1979). Note discussion in Chapter 12: "Is Everything Remembered?"

3. *Ibid.*, pg. 7. Russell states that we probably use even less than 1% of our brains' potential; in his words—"more likely .01% or less!"

4. *Ibid.*, Note discussion in Chapter 4: "The Two Sides of the Brain." Since Sperry's original discoveries about the two sides of the brain, there has been a tremendous explosion of interest in this area. Researchers have found that each hemisphere is actually capable of doing the work of the other, and that the division of function is not as clear as it first seemed. I recommend thinking of the terms 'left-brained' and 'right-brained' as references to the skills of logic and imagination, respectively. Wherever these abilities may be 'located', our highest functioning results from their balanced use.

5. *Ibid.*, Note discussion in Chapter 8: "Imagery And Its Relationship To Memory."

Chapter 2: Map Your Mind

1. Tony Buzan, *Use Both Sides of Your Brain*, op. cit. Note discussion in Chapter 4: "Noting."

2. Betty Edwards, *Drawing on the Right Side of the Brain*, (J.P. Tarcher, Los Angeles, 1979). A brilliant exposition of the 'brain benefits' of drawing.

3. Tony Buzan, *Use Both Sides of Your Brain*, op. cit. Note discussion in Chapter 4: "Noting." See also: Howe and Godfrey, *Student Note Taking as an Aid to Learning.* Exeter University, England, 1977.

Chapter 3: Think of Them

No notes for this chapter.

Chapter 4: Build Their Recall

1. Peter Russell, *The Brain Book*, op. cit. Note Chapter 6: "The Psychology of Memory."

2. *Ibid.*

3. Turk, Christopher, *Effective Speaking: Communicating in Speech.* (E. & F.N. Spon, New York, 1985), pg. 49. Turk states "the listeners must be able to grasp the structure of the talk. Make sure that you make the overall pattern of your presentation plain to the audience."

4. *Ibid.*, pg. 75.

5. Peter Russell, *The Brain Book*, op. cit. Note Chapter 6: "The Psychology of Memory."

6. *Ibid.*

Chapter 5: Perfect Practice

1. A. Richardson, *Mental Imagery*, (Routledge and Kegan Paul, London, 1969), page 56.

2. Peter Russell, *The Brain Book*, op. cit. Chapter 15.

3. I recommend the relaxation exercise taught in Dr. Herbert Benson's book, *The Relaxation Response*, (Collins, London, 1976).

4. John Basmajian, "Conscious Control of Single Nerve Cells," *New Scientist*, December 1963, pg. 663.

Chapter 6: Set Your Stage

1. John Diamond, *Behavioural Kinesiology: the new science for positive health through muscle testing*, (Harper and Row, New York, 1979), pgs. 78-79.

2. Peter Russell, *The Brain Book*, op. cit., page 208.

3. John Diamond, *Behavioural Kinesiology: the new science for positive health through muscle testing,* op. cit. Note discussion in Chapter 9: "The Music in Your Life."

Chapter 7: Transforming Fear

1. Frank Pierce Jones, *Body Awareness in Action, A Study of the Alexander Technique,* (Schocken Books, New York, 1976).

2. F. M. Alexander, *The Use of the Self.* Reprinted by Centerline Press, CA. 1986.

3. This subtle form of manual guidance is unique and has to be experienced to be understood and appreciated.

Chapter 8: Let Your Body Talk

1. Albert Mehrabian, *Silent Messages,* (Wadsworth, U.K. 1971). See also M. Argyle et al, "The Communication of Superior and Inferior Attitudes by Verbal and Non-Verbal Signals," British Journal of Social and Clinical Psychology, Vol. 9 (1970), pgs. 222-231.

2. For information on learning American Sign Language, contact:
National Information Center on Deafness
800 Florida Avenue, N.E.
Washington, D.C. 20002

3. Albert Mehrabian, *Silent Messages,* op. cit.

Chapter 9: Better and Better

1. For further information, contact:

Toastmasters International, Inc.
P.O. Box 10400
Santa Ana, California 92711

National Speakers Association
4747 North Seventh Street
Suite 310
Phoenix, Arizona 85014

Suggested Further Readings

Alexander, F. Mathias, *The Use of the Self*. Reprinted by Centerline Press, CA. 1986. The author's fascinating account of his discovery of the Alexander Technique. Invaluable.

Baker, Elsworth F., *Man in the Trap: The causes of blocked sexual energy*, (Collier Books, New York, 1967). An incisive look at the work of Wilhelm Reich. Baker's book elaborates, with numerous examples, Reich's discoveries of various styles of 'character armor', the study of which offers profound insights for any student of presentation skills.

Bandler, Richard and Grinder, John, *"Frogs into Princes: Neuro Linguistic Programming*, (Real People Press, Utah, 1979). A valuable introductory work on the subject of neuro-linguistic programming: a discipline which explores the fine points of non-verbal communication, as well as different strategies of listening and learning.

Benson, Herbert, *The Relaxation Response*, (Collins, London, 1976). The result of Benson's distillation of a pot pourri of relaxation techniques into one simple, practical method, which can actually be learned from the book.

Buzan, Tony, *Use Both Sides of Your Brain*, (E.P. Dutton, New York, 1985). Buzan's classic work originally published in 1971, established him as the father of 'whole-brain' education. This book is an invaluable guide for anyone interested in learning how to learn and communicate.

Buzan, Tony, *Use Your Memory*, (B.B.C. Publications, London, 1986). The best of the 'how-to' memory books. Buzan deals with the subject comprehensively; his techniques are easy to learn, and immediately applicable.

Diamond, John, *Behavioural Kinesiology: the new science for positive health through muscle testing*, (Harper and Row, New York, 1979). Diamond is a pioneer in the study of the subtle but powerful effects of various environmental factors, such as lighting and music, on audiences.

Dobson, Terry and Miller, Victor, *Attactics: Giving in to Get Your Way,* (Delacorte Press, New York, 1978). This book demonstrates a variety of creative strategies for dealing with conflict in every day life. It is particularly valuable for the presenter interested in learning how to handle 'difficult people'.

Edwards, Betty, *Drawing on the Right Side of the Brain,* (J.P. Tracher, Los Angeles, 1979). Betty Edwards' book has become a classic in the field of whole-brain education. In addition to actually learning how to draw, the careful reader will also gain valuable insights into the role of imagery in thinking and creating.

Ferguson, Marylin, Ed., *The Brain-Mind Bulletin.* (Interface Press, CA). This Bulletin offers well-written abstracts on the latest advances in brain studies. I particularly recommend their reprints on left/right-brain research.

Gardner, Howard, *Frame of Mind: The Theory of Multiple Intelligences,* (Basic Books, New York 1985). Gardner's book elaborates on seven major types of intelligences, and provides a useful perspective on the various styles of learning and listening.

Gelb, Michael, *Body Learning: An Introduction to the Alexander Technique* (Henry Holt and Company, New York, 1987). *Publishers Weekly* called this the most lucid book on the subject.

Hart, Leslie, *How the Brain Works,* (Basic Books, New York, 1975). Leslie Hart provides a fascinating look at the workings of the human brain, emphasizing particularly its active, pattern-seeking nature. Very helpful in understanding the nature of audience recall.

Herrigel, Eugen, *Zen and the Art of Archery,* (Vintage, New York, 1971). This delightful little book offers penetrating insights into the attainment of excellence in any discipline.

Jones, Frank Pierce, *Body Awareness in Action, A Study of the Alexander Technique,* Schocken Books, New York, 1976. This excellent book includes an extensive discussion of Jones' groundbreaking scientific study of the Alexander Technique, including his work on the startle pattern.

Peters, Tom and Austin, Nancy, *A Passion for Excellence* (Warner Books, New York, 1986). A valuable presentation of various corporate 'models of excellence'. This book repeatedly demonstrates the intimate relationship between leadership and effective presentation skills. The section on coaching has particular relevance for those who wish to develop a team approach to improving presentation skills.

Restak, Richard M., *THE BRAIN: The Last Frontier*, (Warner Books, New York, 1979). A thorough, easy to read discussion of brain science.

Rowse, A.L., *The Annotated Shakespeare*, (Greenwich House, Crown Books, New York, 1984). Shakespeare's works provide the ultimate guide to presentation skills.

Russell, Peter, *The Brain Book*, (Routledge and Kegan Paul, London, 1979). This superb text provides the research details behind Buzan's classic "Use Both Sides of Your Brain."

Samples, Bob, *Open Mind/Whole Mind*, (Jalmar Press, Rolling Hills Estates, 1987). A fascinating exploration of how the brain-mind system acquires, processes and expresses experience.

Samuels, M. and Sameuls, N., *Seeing With the Mind's Eye*, (Random House, New York, 1976). This comprehensive work provides fascinating information on the history and uses of visualization.

Selye, Hans, *The Stress of Life*, (McGraw Hill, New York, 1978). This is the original work on stress which introduced the notion of 'fight or flight'.

Turk, Christopher, *Effective Speaking: Communicating in Speech*. (E. & F.N. Spon, New York, 1985). Turk's book is a very well researched, detailed guide to presentation skills. It is, however, unnecessarily limited by its focus on attaining only 'a decent standard of ordinary competence' rather than encouraging its readers to strive for excellence.

For further information on lectures, seminars and consulting services, contact:

High Performance Learning Center
4613 Davenport Street, N.W.
Washington, D.C. 20016
(202) 537-0775

Openmind/Wholemind
Parenting & Teaching Tomorrow's Children Today

A book of powerful possibilities that honors the capacities, capabilities, and potentials of adult and child alike. Uses Modalities, Intelligences, Styles and Creativity to explore how the brain-mind system acquires, processes and expresses experience. Foreword by M. McClaren & C. Charles.
0-915190-45-1 $14.95
7 × 9 paperback
81 B/W photos 29 illus.

Present Yourself! *Captivate Your Audience With Great Presentation Skills*

Become a presenter who is a dynamic part of the message. Learn about Transforming Fear, Knowing Your Audience, Setting The Stage, Making Them Remember and much more. Essential reading for anyone interested in the art of communication. Destined to become the standard work in its field.
0-915190-51-6 paper $9.95
0-915190-50-8 cloth $18.95
6 × 9 paper/cloth. illus.

Unicorns Are Real
A Right-Brained Approach to Learning

Over 100,000 sold. The long-awaited "right hemispheric" teaching strategies developed by popular educational specialist Barbara Vitale are now available. Hemispheric dominance screening instrument included.
0-915190-35-4 $10.95
8½ × 11 paperback, illus.

Unicorns Are Real Poster

Beautifully-illustrated. Guaranteed to capture the fancy of young and old alike. Perfect gift for unicorn lovers, right-brained thinkers and all those who know how to dream.
For classroom, office or home display.
JP9027 $4.95
19 × 27 full color

Imagination is the unicorn that lifts us above the mundane chains that bind the minds of many and flies us on fantastic wings to a place where dreams DO come true.

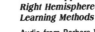

Practical Application, Right Hemisphere Learning Methods

Audio from Barbara Vitale. Discover many practical ways to successfully teach right-brained students using whole-to-part learning, visualization activities, color stimuli, motor skill techniques and more.
JP9110 $12.95
Audio Cassette

Don't Push Me, I'm Learning as Fast as I Can

Barbara Vitale presents some remarkable insights on the physical growth stages of children and how these stages affect a child's ability, not only to learn, but to function in the classroom.

JP9112 $12.95
Audio Cassette

Tapping Our Untapped Potential

This Barbara Vitale tape gives new insights on how you process information. Will help you develop strategies for improving memory, fighting stress and organizing your personal and professional activities.

JP9111 $12.95
Audio Cassette

Free Flight *Celebrating Your Right Brain*

Journey with Barbara Vitale, from her uncertain childhood perceptions of being "different" to the acceptance and adult celebration of that difference. A book for right-brained people in a left-brained world. Foreword by Bob Samples.
0-915190-44-3 $8.95
5½ × 8½ paperback, illus.

"He Hit Me Back First"
Self-Esteem through Self-Discipline

Simple techniques for guiding children toward self-correcting behavior as they become aware of choice and their own inner authority.
0-915190-36-2 $10.95
8½ × 11 paperback, illus.

Learning To Live, Learning To Love

An inspirational message about the importance of love in everything we do. Beautifully told through words and pictures. Ageless and timeless.

0-915190-38-9 $7.95
6 × 9 paperback, illus.

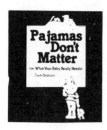

Pajamas Don't Matter:
(or What Your Baby Really Needs)

Here's help for new parents everywhere! Provides valuable information and needed reassurances to new parents as they struggle through the frantic, but rewarding, first years of their child's life.
0-915190-21-4　　$5.95
8½ × 11　paperback, full color

From Two To Three Years:
Social Competence

Shows important ways children define their identity by learning to play with other children, exploring the world, mastering the art of communication, and developing their senses of imagination and humor.

0-935266-03-8　　$5.95
8½ × 11　paper, B/W photos

Feelings Alphabet

Brand-new kind of alphabet book full of photos and word graphics that will delight readers of all ages.''...lively, candid...the 26 words of this pleasant book express experiences common to all children.'' *Library Journal*
0-935266-15-1　　$5.95
6 × 9　paperback, B/W photos

The Parent Book

A functional and sensitive guide for parents who want to enjoy every minute of their child's growing years. Shows how to live with children in ways that encourage healthy emotional development. Ages 3-14.

0-915190-15-X　　$9.95
8½ × 11　paperback, illus.

Aliens In My Nest
SQUIB Meets The Teen Creature

Squib comes home from summer camp to find that his older brother, Andrew, has turned into a snarly, surly, defiant, and non-communicative adolescent. *Aliens* explores the effect of Andrew's new behavior on Squib and the entire family unit.
0-915190-49-4　　$7.95
8½ × 11　paperback, illus.

Hugs & Shrugs
The Continuing Saga of SQUIB

Squib feels incomplete. He has lost a piece of himself. He searches every where only to discover that his missing pieces has fallen in and not out. He becomes complete again once he discovers his own inner-peace.

0-915190-47-8　　$7.95
8½ × 11　paperback, illus.

Moths & Mothers/ Feather & Fathers
A Story About a Tiny Owl Named SQUIB

Squib is a tiny owl who cannot fly. Neither can he understand his feelings. He must face the frustration, grief, fear, guilt and loneliness that we all must face at different times in our lives. Struggling with these feelings, he searches, at least, for understanding.

0-395-36555-4　　$7.95
8½ × 11　paperback, illus.

Hoots & Toots & Hairy Brutes
The Continuing Adventures of SQUIB

Squib—who can only toot—sets out to learn how to give a mighty hoot. His attempts result in abject failure. Every reader who has struggled with life's limitations will recognize their own struggles and triumphs in the microcosm of Squib's forest world. A parable for all ages from 8 to 80.
0-395-39503-8　　$7.95
8½ × 11　paperback, illus.

The Turbulent Teens
Understanding Helping Surviving

''This book should be read by every parent of a teenager in America...It gives a parent the information needed to understand teenagers and guide them wisely.''—Dr. Fitzhugh Dodson, author of *How to Parent, How to Father, and How to Discipline with Love.*
0-913091-01-4　　$8.95
6 × 9　paperback.

Whose Child Cries
Children of Gay Parents Talk About Their Lives

Straightforward and heartfelt explanations help make this book a valuable resource on homosexuality.

Foreword by Eda LeShan, columnist for Woman's Day Magazine.

0-915190-39-7　paperback $8.95
0-915190-40-0　cloth $16.95
5½ × 8½　paperback/cloth

Learning The Skills of Peacemaking
An Activity Guide for Elementary-Age Children

"Global peace begins with you. Guide develops this fundamental concept in fifty lessons. If this curriculum was a required course in every elementary school in every country, we would see world peace in our children's lifetimes." — *Letty Cottin Pogrebin*, Ms. Magazine
0-915190-46-X $17.95
8½ × 11 paperback, illus.

Project Self-Esteem
A Parent Involvement Program for Elementary-Age Children

An innovative parent-support program that promotes children's self-worth. "Project Self Esteem is the most extensively tested and affordable drug and alcohol preventative program available."

0-935266-16-X $24.95
8½ × 11 paperback, illus.

PSE Workshop Video Tape

Provide special training for your PSE team. Includes:
- Background Information
- Importance of Self-Esteem
- Program Philosophy & Implementation
- Full Lesson Demonstration
- Classroom Presentations
- Tips on Working with Children

BW6689 $149.95
½" VHS 1½hrs.

Reading, Writing and Rage

An autopsy of one profound school failure, disclosing the complex processes behind it and the secret rage that grew out of it.

Must reading for anyone working with learning disabled, functional illiterates, or juvenile delinquents.

0-915190-42-7 $12.95
5½ × 8½ paperback

A System For Caring
Supportive Counseling Techniques for Professionals and Families

Here is a book, devoted to caring and helping, that presents an orderly, simple sequence of techniques for supporting those who are hurting. Use these skills in your personal or professional life and feel enriched by the gratitude and affection of those you have helped.
0-915190-55-9 $9.95
6 × 9 paperback, illus.

Esteem Builders

You CAN improve your students' behavior and achievement through building self-esteem. Here is a book packed with classroom-proven techniques, activities, and ideas you can immediately use in your own program or at home.

Ideas, ideas, ideas, for grades K-8 and parents.

0-915190-53-2 $24.95
8½ × 11 paperback, illus.

Social Acceptance: Key To Mainstreaming

Helps teachers become good role models for the understanding and acceptance of self and others. A must for teachers concerned with the social and emotional development of students in their classroom. Gr. K-8.
0-935266-05-4 $5.95
8½ × 11 saddle-stitched, illus.

Communicating to Make Friends

Focuses on changing young people's attitudes toward the handicapped, minority, withdrawn, or gifted student. Exciting activities help discover commonalities. Thoroughly tested. Gr. K-6.
0-935266-04-6 $9.95
8½ × 11 paperback, illus.

Unlocking Doors To Friendship

Presents innovative ideas to make the secondary classroom a more positive learning experience—socially and emotionally—for students and teachers. Over 100 lesson plans included. Designed for easy infusion into curriculum. Gr. 7-12.
0-935266-14-3 $14.95
6 × 9 paperback, illus.

SAGE: Self-Awareness Growth Experiences

A veritable treasure trove of activities and strategies promoting positive behavior and meeting the personal/social needs of young people in grades 7-12. Organized around affective learning goals and objectives. Over 150 activities.
0-935266-08-9 $14.95
6 × 9 paperback, illus.

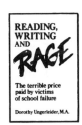